KNITTING 24/7

30 Projects to Knit, Wear, and Enjoy, On the Go and Around the Clock

HATS, SCARVES, SOCKS, BAGS, MITTS, AND MORE FOR BUSY, PASSIONATE KNITTERS

VÉRONIK AVERY

Photographs by Thayer Allyson Gowdy

Styling by Karen Schaupeter

STC CRAFT | A MELANIE FALICK BOOK   NEW YORK

Published in 2010 by Stewart, Tabori & Chang
An imprint of ABRAMS

Library of Congress Cataloging-in-Publication Data:
Avery, Véronik.
Knitting 24/7 / by Véronik Avery ; photographs by Thayer Allyson Gowdy.
   p. cm.
ISBN 978-1-58479-844-6
1. Knitting—Patterns. 2. Dress accessories. 3. Sweaters. I. Title.
II. Title: Knitting twenty-four seven.
TT825.A845 2010
746.43 ' 2041 —dc22
   2009029919

Editor: Liana Allday
Designer: Anna Christian
Production Manager: Jacqueline Poirier

The text of this book was composed in Shinn and Promemoria.

Printed and bound in China

10 9 8 7 6 5 4 3 2 1

Stewart, Tabori & Chang books are available at special discounts when
purchased in quantity for premiums and promotions as well as fundraising
or educational use. Special editions can also be created to specification.
For details, contact specialsales@abramsbooks.com or the address below.

ABRAMS
THE ART OF BOOKS SINCE 1949

115 West 18th Street
New York, NY 10011
www.abramsbooks.com

For Marcel

CONTENTS

27
30
33
41
43
37
47

67
71
74
77
79
81
81

101
105
109
111
113
117

INTRODUCTION

Monday, 3 p.m.: One woman is squeezing in an extra errand before picking up her children at school, another sprints to a meeting, while a third leads a yoga class. They all have different, busy schedules, but they're all passionate knitters, determined to find time to knit.

I relate to these women—as a knitwear designer, writer, and mother, I'm often multitasking and, in the midst of it all, I like to knit as much as I can. In fact, I always take a project with me wherever I go, just in case I am able to find a few minutes to work a few rows. The truth is I'd like to be knitting 24/7—that is, all the time. When I have a project in my bag, I don't even mind a long commute or having to wait in line—in fact, I even get excited knowing that a stretch of uninterrupted knitting time awaits me.

I often have many projects going at once, but I make sure they are diverse in size and complexity to suit a variety of circumstances. For instance, I have the luxury of space while I'm at home and don't mind if my project takes over the couch and the coffee table, but a sprawling project like this won't work on the subway. And just as I wouldn't wear mittens in July, I wouldn't knit a heavy wool shawl poolside during the summer. Similarly, I wouldn't take a multicolored yoked sweater to one of the very social knit nights that I enjoy with my friends.

I designed the projects in *Knitting 24/7* to be portable and to make use of our "extra" time—those nooks and crannies in our lives when we are busy, yet our hands are free to practice our craft. Many of us like to knit while we travel, wait, watch, or listen, and times like these call for projects that can be easily stowed in a bag and contained in our laps. They also call for easily memorized stitch patterns so that charts are not needed once the pattern has been established. For instance, the lace pattern in the Arrowhead Kneesocks (page 47) requires only a 4-round repeat, and the complex appearance of the diagonal mesh in the Linen Market Bag (page 71) is created by working a very simple openwork pattern and then repositioning the beginning-of-round stitch marker every sixth round. Projects like the Fleur de Lys Hat (page 87) include colorwork, but with only two different shades of yarn to avoid tangles.

Almost every project in this book is small and can be completed quickly, giving even the busiest knitter a sense of accomplishment. Plus small knitted items are perfect gifts that are universally beloved, and at the same time require little yarn. I also included a few larger projects that I consider "mindless knitting" for times when there is room for a bigger project but one's focus cannot be on a chart or stitch pattern. Circular knitting is one of my favorite ways to knit mindlessly. The Elemental Pullover (page 67), for example, is knitted circularly from the bottom up in Stockinette stitch, providing hours of easy knitting during which the mind is free to wander. The Fir Cone Shrug (page 61) is an example of mindless back-and-forth knitting, calling for an easy-to-memorize stitch pattern and serving as a lap blanket while being knitted.

All of the projects in *Knitting 24/7* are stylish and functional because, in addition to wanting to find as much time to knit as possible, most of us want to look as good as we can all the time—be it a morning at work, a dinner with friends, or a relaxing weekend afternoon. For that reason I have organized the patterns into a.m., p.m., and weekend, as these are often the categories that define our wardrobes. These pieces are classic yet feminine and provide a wealth of options for our varying needs from the time we wake until we go to bed. I hope that this blend of projects—delicate stoles, warm scarves, pretty gloves, jaunty caps, vests, shrugs, and so on—will help you keep your needles clicking and your wardrobe special, no matter how much or how little time you have to knit.

Veronik Avery

SNEAK IN A FEW ROWS

—before breakfast

—before kids get up

—while coffee brews

—while watching weather report

—on subway

—waiting for yoga class to begin

—while computer warms up

—in line at DMV

—between meetings

—in doctor's office

a.m.

PATTERNED MITTENS

While the idea for some knitted items begins with the yarn, these mittens were inspired by a hand-printed abstract fabric designed by Gudrun Sjödén. I received a pouch made from this fabric as a giveaway from *Selvedge* magazine, and I found the color combination—charcoal and green spiced up with yellow and pink—so appealing that I knew I had to find a project for it. I incorporated the palette into this pair of modern mittens with a simple striped Garter cuff and slipped-stitch patterning on the hand.

NOTES

When changing colors in Garter Stripe Pattern, leave old color hanging in back, bring new color from below, over old color and to the back before slipping the first st and knitting the second.

STITCH PATTERN

Garter Stripe Pattern
(any number of sts; 4-row repeat)
Row 1: With A, slip 1, knit to end.
Rows 2 and 3: With B, slip 1, knit to end.
Row 4: Repeat Row 1.
Repeat Rows 1–4 for Garter Stripe Pattern.

LEFT MITTEN
CUFF

Using waste yarn and provisional CO of your choice, CO 32 sts. Change to A and Garter Stripe Pattern; work Rows 1–4 twenty-three (25, 27) times, then work Rows 1 and 2 once.

Carefully remove waste yarn from CO and place sts on needle. Using Kitchener st (see Special Techniques, page 122) and A, graft last row to CO row.

HAND

With RS of Cuff facing, using A, beginning at graft, pick up and knit 1 st for every Garter st ridge along side edge of Cuff—48 (52, 56) sts. Join for working in the rnd; place marker (pm) for beginning of rnd. Purl 1 rnd. Knit 2 rnds.

Next Rnd: *K1, M1, k5 (6, 7), [M1, k6] twice, M1, k5 (6, 7), M1, k1*, pm for side, repeat from * to * once—58 (62, 66) sts. Knit 2 rnds.

Begin Slip Stitch Pattern: Work Slip Stitch Pattern from Chart to first marker, beginning and ending Chart as indicated for your size, work in St st (knit every rnd) to end, working St st

FINISHED MEASUREMENTS
Approximately 7 (7 ½, 8)" hand circumference

YARN
Harrisville Designs New England Shetland (100% wool; 217 yards / 50 grams): 1 hank each #7 Tundra (A), #49 Charcoal (B), #34 Aster (C), and #6 Cornsilk (D)

NEEDLES
One set of five double-pointed needles (dpn) size US 1 (2.25 mm) Change needle size if necessary to obtain correct gauge.

NOTIONS
Stitch markers (one in contrasting color for beginning of rnd); waste yarn

GAUGE
25 sts and 32 rnds = 3" (7.5 cm) in Slip Stitch Pattern from Chart

SLIP STITCH PATTERN

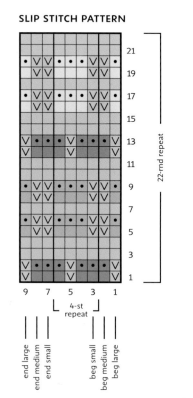

KEY

☐ Knit

⊡ Purl

▽ Slip 1

☐ A

■ B

☐ C

☐ D

22-rnd repeat

4-st repeat

end large
end medium
end small
beg small
beg medium
beg large

across bottom sts, pick up and knit 2 sts at other side of Thumb Opening, knit across top sts—21 (23, 25) sts. Redistribute sts evenly among 3 dpns. Join for working in the rnd; pm for beginning of rnd. Begin St st; work even until Thumb measures 1 ¾ (2, 2)″, or almost covers thumb.

Decrease Rnd 1: *K2tog; repeat from * to last st, k1—11 (12, 13) sts remain.

Decrease Rnd 2: *K2tog; repeat from * to last 1 (0, 1) st(s), k1 (0, 1)—6 (6, 7) sts remain. Cut yarn, leaving a 6″ tail. Thread tail through remaining sts, pull tight and fasten off.

RIGHT MITTEN
Work as for Left Mitten to beginning of Slip Stitch Pattern.

Begin Slip Stitch Pattern: Work in St st to first marker, working in same color as worked in Chart, work in Slip Stitch Pattern from Chart to end, beginning and ending Chart as indicated for your size. Work even until piece measures 2 ¾ (3, 3 ¼)″ from pick-up rnd.

THUMB OPENING
Next Rnd: Change to waste yarn and k9 (10, 11), slip these 9 (10, 11) sts back to left-hand needle, change to working yarn, knit these 9 (10, 11) sts again, work to end. Complete as for Left Mitten.

FINISHING
Block as desired.

in same color as worked in Chart. Work even until piece measures 2 ¾ (3, 3 ¼)″ from pick-up rnd.

THUMB OPENING
Next Rnd: Work to last 9 (10, 11) sts, change to waste yarn and knit to end, slip these 9 (10, 11) sts back to left-hand needle, change to working yarn, knit these 9 (10, 11) sts again. Work even until piece measures 5 ½ (6 ¼, 6 ½)″ from pick-up rnd, or to 1 ¼ (1 ½, 1 ½)″ less than desired length.

MITTEN TOP
Decrease Rnd: Decrease 4 sts this rnd, every other rnd 5 times, then every rnd 3 (4, 5) times, as follows: [K1, ssk, work to 3 sts before next marker, k2tog, k1] twice—22 sts remain. Divide sts evenly onto 2 needles. Using Kitchener st, graft sts.

THUMB
Carefully remove waste yarn from Thumb sts and place bottom 9 (10, 11) sts and top 8 (9, 10) sts onto 2 dpns, being careful not to twist sts. Join C to bottom sts, pick up and knit 2 sts at side of Thumb Opening, knit

CROSS-STITCH LOUNGE SOCKS

Though a thick sock like this is typically worn with boots, a touch of angora makes this is a true luxury sock—best enjoyed while lounging in a bathrobe, not on a mountaintop. The technique for the cable pattern used in these socks is a little unusual. Instead of crossing stitches in front of or behind one another, as is usually done for cables, two stitches are passed *through* another pair of stitches. To make this process easy, the stitches are enlarged on the preceding row by wrapping the yarn twice around the needle for each stitch that will be passed through another.

STITCH PATTERNS

3x3 Rib
(multiple of 6 sts; 1-rnd repeat)
All Rnds: P2, *k3, p3; repeat from * to last 4 sts, k3, p1.

Cross-Stitch Cables
(multiple of 6 sts; 4-rnd repeat)
Rnd 1: *P1, k4, p1; repeat from * to end.
Rnd 2: *P1, [k1, wrapping yarn twice] 4 times, p1; repeat from * to end.
Rnd 3: *P1, slip 4 wyib, dropping extra wraps; with left-hand needle, slip first 2 sts over second 2 sts onto left-hand needle (sts are now crossed), slip remaining 2 sts from right-hand needle back to left-hand needle, knit these 4 sts in their new crossed position, p1; repeat from * to end.
Rnd 4: Repeat Rnd 1.
Repeat Rnds 1–4 for Cross-Stitch Cables.

LEG

CO 48 sts. Distribute sts evenly among 4 needles. Join for working in the rnd, being careful not to twist sts; place marker (pm) for beginning of rnd. Begin 3x3 Rib; work even for 1½".

Next Rnd: *P2tog, k1, M1, k2, p1; repeat from * to end.

Next Rnd: Change to Cross-Stitch Cables; work even until piece measures approximately 8" from the beginning, ending with Rnd 1, 3, or 4 of pattern.

HEEL FLAP

Set-Up Row 1 (RS): Change to smaller needles. K12, turn.

Set-Up Row 2: Slip 1, p23, working all 24 sts onto 1 needle for Heel Flap, and removing marker. Leave remaining 24 sts on 2 needles for instep.

SIZES

To fit women's shoe sizes 6–10

FINISHED MEASUREMENTS

▸ 8" Foot circumference
▸ 8½" Foot length from back of Heel
▸ 9½" Leg length to base of Heel

YARN

Naturally Sensation (70% merino wool / 30% angora; 131 yards / 50 grams): 2 hanks #304 Grape

NEEDLES

▸ One set of five double-pointed needles (dpn) size US 3 (3.25 mm)
▸ One set of five double-pointed needles size US 2 (2.75 mm)
Change needle size if necessary to obtain correct gauge.

NOTIONS

Stitch marker

GAUGE

21 sts and 34 rnds = 4" (10 cm) in Stockinette stitch (St st), using larger needles

Row 1: Working only on 24 Heel Flap sts, *slip 1, k1; repeat from * to end.

Row 2: Slip 1, purl to end.

Repeat Rows 1 and 2 ten times.

Turn Heel

Set-Up Row 1 (RS): Change to larger needles. Slip 1, k13, k2tog-tbl, k1, turn.

Set-Up Row 2: Slip 1, p5, p2tog, p1, turn.

Row 1: Slip 1, knit to 1 st before gap, k2tog-tbl (the 2 sts on either side of gap), k1, turn.

Row 2: Slip 1, purl to 1 st before gap, p2tog (the 2 sts on either side of gap), p1, turn.

Repeat Rows 1 and 2 three times, omitting the final k1 and p1 sts in the last repeat of Rows 1 and 2—14 sts remain.

Gusset

Next Row (RS): *Needle 1:* Slip 1, knit across Heel Flap sts, pick up and knit 12 sts along left side of Heel Flap, pick up and knit 1 st from row below first st on Needle 2; *Needles 2 and 3:* Continue Cross-Stitch Cables pattern as established; *Needle 4:* Pick up and knit 1 st from row below first Heel Flap st, pick up and knit 12 sts along left side of Heel Flap, k7 from Needle 1. Join for working in the rnd; pm for beginning of rnd—64 sts (20-12-12-20).

Decrease Rnd: *Needle 1:* Knit to last 2 sts, k2tog; *Needles 2 and 3:* Work even as established; *Needle 4:* Ssk, knit to end—62 sts remain. Work even for 1 rnd.

Repeat Decrease Rnd every other rnd 7 times—48 sts remain (12-12-12-12).

FOOT

Work even until Foot measures 2″ less than desired length from back of Heel.

Next Rnd: K12, p24, k12. Knit 3 rnds.

TOE

Decrease Rnd: *Needle 1:* Knit to last 3 sts, k2tog, k1; *Needle 2:* K1, ssk, knit to end; *Needle 3:* Knit to last 3 sts, k2tog, k1; *Needle 4:* K1, ssk, knit to end—44 sts remain. Knit 1 rnd.

Repeat Decrease Rnd every other rnd 4 times, then every rnd 4 times—12 sts remain. Knit to end of Needle 1.

FINISHING

Break yarn, leaving long tail. Transfer sts from Needle 1 to Needle 4, and sts from Needle 3 to Needle 2. Using Kitchener st (see Special Techniques, page 122), graft Toe sts.

Block as desired.

OLIVE HEATHER SKIRT

This skirt is all about versatility—dress it up for the workplace with a tailored jacket or make it playful with a printed blouse for a casual date. And because it is worked in the round from the bottom up, the skirt has no side seams, meaning that it has no true front and back. Wear it as you will, with the decorative slanted lines meeting along the sides or along the center.

ABBREVIATIONS

d2r (right-leaning double decrease): Slip 2 sts to cn, hold to back, [k2tog (1 st on left-hand needle together with 1 st on cn)] twice.

d2l (left-leaning double decrease): Slip 2 sts to cn, hold to front, [k2tog (1 st on cn together with 1 st on left-hand needle)] twice.

STITCH PATTERN

2x2 Rib

(multiple of 4 sts; 1-rnd repeat)
All Rnds: P1, *k2, p2; repeat from * to last st, p1.

HEM

CO 152 (168, 184, 200, 216, 232, 248) sts. Join for working in the rnd, being careful not to twist sts; place marker (pm) for beginning of rnd. Begin 2x2 Rib; work even for 6 rnds.

Begin Diagonal Bands: K3, pm, [p2, k13 (14, 15, 17, 18, 19, 21)] 3 times, p2, k52 (62, 72, 76, 86, 96, 100), pm, [p2, k13 (14, 15, 17, 18, 19, 21)] 3 times, p2, knit to end.

Next Rnd: Knit the knit sts and purl the purl sts as they face you. Work even for 8 rnds.

Shift Bands: Shift bands this rnd, then every 10 rnds 7 (9, 9, 9, 9, 9, 9) times, as follows: Knit to 2 sts before first marker, [k1-b/f] twice, slip marker (sm), [p2, d2r, k7 (8, 9, 11, 12, 13, 15), k1-b/f, k1-b/f] 3 times, p2, d2r, knit to 4 sts before next marker, d2l, sm, [p2, k1-b/f, k1-b/f, k7 (8, 9, 11, 12, 13, 15), d2l] 3 times, p2, [k1-b/f] twice, knit to end. Work even for 9 rnds.

Shape Waist

Decrease Rnd 1: Decrease 4 sts this rnd, then every 10 rnds once, as follows: Knit to first marker, sm, [p2, d2r, k7 (8, 9, 11, 12, 13, 15), k1-b/f, k1-b/f] 3 times, p2, d2r, knit to 4 sts before next marker, d2l, sm, [p2, k1-b/f, k1-b/f, k7 (8, 9, 11, 12, 13, 15), d2l] 3 times, p2, knit to end— 144 (160, 176, 192, 208, 224, 240) sts remain. Work even for 9 rnds.

SIZES

X-Small (Small, Medium, Large, 1X-Large, 2X-Large, 3X-Large)

FINISHED MEASUREMENTS

30 ½ (33 ½, 36 ¾, 40, 43 ¼, 46 ½, 49 ½)" hip
For best fit, select a size 3–4" smaller than your actual hip measurement.

YARN

Cascade Yarns Cascade 220 Heathers (100% Peruvian highland wool; 220 yards / 100 grams): 3 (3, 3, 4, 4, 4, 5) hanks #9448 Olive Heather

NEEDLES

One 24" (60 cm) long or longer circular (circ) needle size US 6 (4 mm)
Change needle size if necessary to obtain correct gauge.

NOTIONS

Stitch markers (one in contrasting color for beginning of rnd); cable needle (cn)

GAUGE

20 sts and 31 rnds = 4" (10 cm) in Stockinette stitch (St st)

Decrease Rnd 2: Knit to 2 sts before first marker, [k1-b/f] twice, sm, [p2, d2r, k9 (10, 11, 13, 14, 15, 17)] 3 times, p2, d2r, knit to 4 sts before next marker, d2l, sm, [p2, k9 (10, 11, 13, 14, 15, 17), d2l] 3 times, p2, [k1-b/f] twice, knit to end—132 (148, 164, 180, 196, 212, 228) sts remain. Work even for 9 rnds.

Decrease Rnd 3: Knit to 2 sts before first marker, [k1-b/f] twice, sm, [p2, d2r, k7 (8, 9, 11, 12, 13, 15)] 3 times, p2, d2r, knit to 4 sts before next marker, d2l, sm, [p2, k7 (8, 9, 11, 12, 13, 15), d2l] 3 times, p2, [k1-b/f] twice, knit to end—120 (136, 152, 168, 184, 200, 216) sts remain. Work even for 7 rnds.

Waistband: Change to 2x2 Rib; work even for 6 rnds. BO all sts in pattern.

FINISHING
Block as desired.

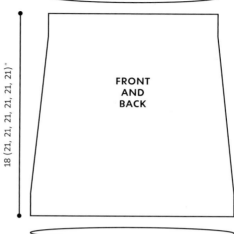

24 (27 1/4, 30 1/2, 33 1/2, 36 3/4, 40, 43 1/4)"

18 (21, 21, 21, 21, 21, 21)"

FRONT
AND
BACK

30 1/2 (33 1/2, 36 3/4, 40, 43 1/4, 46 1/2, 49 1/2)"

GRANDFATHER VEST

Styled after a classic menswear piece, this warm, soft angora vest can be worn casually around the house, but would easily spruce up any workday outfit. Because it is knitted in the round, it is a great project to work on when your attention must be elsewhere, with the added benefit of no seams to sew at the end.

STITCH PATTERN

2x2 Rib

(multiple of 4 sts)

All Rnds: *K2, p2; repeat from * to end.

BODY

Using longer circ needle, CO 172 (192, 212, 232, 252, 272) sts. Join for working in the rnd, being careful not to twist sts; place marker (pm) for beginning of rnd. Begin 2x2 Rib; work even until piece measures 2″ from the beginning. Change to St st (knit every rnd); work even until piece measures 2 ¾″ from the beginning.

Next Rnd: K86 (96, 106, 116, 126, 136), pm for right side, knit to end.

Shape Waist: Decrease 4 sts this rnd, then every 10 rnds 4 times, as follows: [Ssk, knit to 2 sts before marker, k2tog] twice—152 (172, 192, 212, 232, 252) sts remain. Work even until piece measures 11 ¾″ from the beginning.

Shape Bust: Increase 4 sts this rnd, then every 10 rnds once, as follows: [K1, M1, knit to 1 st before marker,

M1, k1] twice—160 (180, 200, 220, 240, 260) sts. Work even until piece measures 14 ½ (14 ½, 14 ½, 15 ½, 15 ½, 15 ½)″ from the beginning, ending 6 (8, 9, 10, 12, 14) sts before end of rnd.

Divide for Fronts and Back: K12 (16, 18, 20, 24, 28) and place sts on holder for left underarm, k31 (34, 38, 42, 45, 48) and place sts on holder for Left Front, k6 and place sts on holder for center Front neck, k31 (34, 38, 42, 45, 48) and place sts on holder for Right Front, k12 (16, 18, 20, 24, 28) and place sts on holder for right underarm, knit to end—68 (74, 82, 90, 96, 102) sts remain for Back.

BACK

Working only on Back sts, purl 1 WS row.

Shape Armholes (RS): Decrease 1 st each side this row, then every other row 6 (7, 9, 10, 11, 13) times, as follows: K2, k2tog, knit to last 4 sts, ssk, k2—54 (58, 62, 68, 72, 74) sts remain. Work even until armhole measures 7 ¾ (8 ¼, 8 ¾, 9, 9 ¼, 9 ¼)″, ending with a WS row.

SIZES

X-Small (Small, Medium, Large, 1X-Large, 2X-Large)

FINISHED MEASUREMENTS

32 (36, 40, 44, 48, 52)″ bust

YARN

Classic Elite Yarns Lush (50% angora / 50% wool; 123 yards / 50 grams): 5 (6, 7, 8, 8, 9) hanks #4457 Blueberry

NEEDLES

▶ One 24″ (60 cm) long circular (circ) needle size US 7 (4.5 mm)
▶ One 16″ (40 cm) long circular needle size US 7 (4.5 mm)
Change needle size if necessary to obtain correct gauge.

NOTIONS

Stitch markers (one in contrasting color for beginning of rnd); stitch holders; two ¾″ buttons

GAUGE

20 sts and 29 rnds = 4″ (10 cm) in Stockinette stitch (St st)

Next Row (RS): K5 (6, 7, 9, 10, 10), join a second ball of yarn, k44 (46, 48, 50, 52, 54) and place sts on holder for Back neck, knit to end. Working both sides at the same time, work even for 1 row.

Shape Neck (RS): Right neck edge: Knit to last 3 sts, ssk, k1; left neck edge: K1, k2tog, knit to end—4 (5, 6, 8, 9, 9) sts remain each side. Work even until armhole measures 9 (9 ½, 10, 10 ¼, 10 ½, 10 ½)", ending with a WS row. Place sts on holders.

LEFT FRONT

Rejoin yarn to sts on holder for Left Front. Purl 1 WS row.

Shape Armhole (RS): Decrease 1 st at armhole edge this row, then every other row 6 (7, 9, 10, 11, 13) times, as follows: K2, k2tog, knit to end. AT THE SAME TIME, when armhole measures 2 ½", ending with a WS row, begin neck decreases.

Shape Neck (RS): Decrease 1 st at neck edge this row, then every other row 19 (20, 21, 22, 23, 24) times, as follows: Knit to last 4 sts, ssk, k2—4 (5, 6, 8, 9, 9) sts remain after all shaping is complete. Work even until armhole measures 9 (9 ½, 10, 10 ¼, 10 ½, 10 ½)", ending with a WS row. Place sts on holder.

RIGHT FRONT

Rejoin yarn to sts on holder for Right Front. Purl 1 WS row.

Shape Armhole (RS): Decrease 1 st at armhole edge this row, then every other row 6 (7, 9, 10, 11, 13) times, as follows: Knit to last 4 sts, ssk, knit to end. AT THE SAME TIME, when armhole measures 2 ½", ending with a WS row, begin neck decreases.

Shape Neck (RS): Decrease 1 st at neck edge this row, then every other row 19 (20, 21, 22, 23, 24) times, as follows: K2, k2tog, knit to end—4 (5,

6, 8, 9, 9) sts remain after all shaping is complete. Work even until armhole measures 9 (9 ½, 10, 10 ¼, 10 ½, 10 ½)", ending with a WS row. Place sts on holder.

FINISHING

Using Three-Needle BO (see Special Techniques, page 122), join shoulders.

Armhole Edging: With RS facing, transfer last 6 (8, 9, 10, 12, 14)

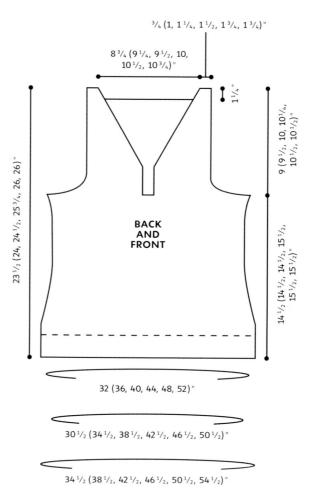

¾ (1, 1 ¼, 1 ½, 1 ¾, 1 ¾)"

8 ¾ (9 ¼, 9 ½, 10, 10 ½, 10 ¾)"

1 ¼"

9 (9 ½, 10, 10 ¼, 10 ½, 10 ½)"

23 ½ (24, 24 ½, 25 ¾, 26, 26)"

BACK AND FRONT

14 ½ (14 ½, 14 ½, 15 ½, 15 ½, 15 ½)"

32 (36, 40, 44, 48, 52)"

30 ½ (34 ½, 38 ½, 42 ½, 46 ½, 50 ½)"

34 ½ (38 ½, 42 ½, 46 ½, 50 ½, 54 ½)"

underarm sts from holder to smaller circ needle. Knit these sts, pick up and knit 96 (100, 110, 112, 116, 116) sts evenly spaced to base of underarm, k6 (8, 9, 10, 12, 14) remaining underarm sts from holder—108 (116, 128, 132, 140, 144) sts. Purl 1 rnd. Change to 2x2 Rib; work even for 6 rnds. BO all sts.

Neckband: With RS facing, pick up and knit 50 (53, 58, 59, 62, 61) sts along Right Front neck edge, 6 sts along right Back neck edge, knit across 44 (46, 48, 50, 52, 54) sts on hold for Back neck, pick up and knit 6 sts along left Back neck edge, and 50 (53, 58, 59, 62, 61) sts along Left Front neck edge—156 (164, 176, 180, 188, 188) sts. Do not join. Knit 1 WS row.

Row 1 (RS): K3, *p2, k2; rep from * to last st, k1.

Row 2: Knit the knit sts and purl the purl sts as they face you. Work even for 2 rows.

Buttonhole Row (RS): K3, yo, p2tog, k2, p2, k2, yo, p2tog, work to end. Work even for 3 rows. BO all sts in pattern.

Using Kitchener st (see Special Techniques, page 122), graft center front neck sts from holder to right edge of Neckband. Sew left edge of Neckband to WS. Sew buttons opposite buttonholes.

Block as desired.

TRANSITIONAL SCARF

Intended to be worn between seasons, this scarf is worked in a cool combination of cotton and Tencel (the latter, a cousin of rayon, boasts both the softness of silk and the strength of polyester). The scarf is worked in two pieces that are joined at the center back neck, which causes the design to run in the same direction on both sides of the body when worn.

FIRST HALF

With straight needles, CO 33 sts loosely. Knit 8 rows. Change to Lace Pattern from Chart; work Rows 1–8 of Chart 27 times. Cut yarn, leaving a 12″ tail. Transfer sts to st holder.

SECOND HALF

Work as for First Half. Transfer sts to dpn, then transfer First Half sts from st holder to second dpn.

FINISHING

With RSs together, holding needle with Second Half sts to the back, join the Halves as follows: *With yarn between needles, slip first st on front (First Half) needle knitwise, then purl first st on back (Second Half) needle*, psso; rep from * to *, then pass first 2 sts on right-hand needle over purled st. Continue in this manner, passing the first 2 sts over the purled st, until all sts have been BO.

Block as desired.

FINISHED MEASUREMENTS

6 ″ wide x 66 ″ long, before blocking

YARN

Classic Elite Yarns Premiere (50% pima cotton / 50% Tencel; 108 yards / 50 grams): 3 hanks #5226 Tidal Wave

NEEDLES

▸ One pair straight needles size US 4 (3.5 mm)
▸ One pair double-pointed needles (dpn) size US 4 (3.5 mm)
Change needle size if necessary to obtain correct gauge.

NOTIONS

Stitch holder

GAUGE

23 sts and 27 rows = 4 ″ (10 cm) in Lace Pattern from Chart

LACE PATTERN

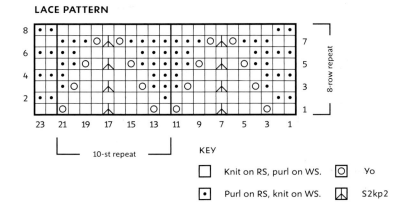

8-row repeat

10-st repeat

KEY

☐ Knit on RS, purl on WS.

⊡ Purl on RS, knit on WS.

Ⓞ Yo

⋀ S2kp2

TRAVEL SHAWL

A shawl is an ideal travel mate; all at once it can be an accessory, a blanket, or a pillow. The easy stitches in the center of this shawl create a delicate field of openwork texture that is then surrounded by a sturdier sawtooth border. The yarn I chose is durable and gets softer with each washing—a perfect combination for an item that will spend a lot of time next to your skin.

ABBREVIATION

M1-u (make 1 untwisted): With tip of left-hand needle inserted from front to back, lift strand between two needles onto left-hand needle; knit strand through front loop to increase 1 st without twisting it.

SHAWL

Using waste yarn, CO 8 sts. Knit 2 rows. Change to working yarn, leaving a 12″ tail; knit 1 row. Join for working in the rnd, being careful not to twist sts; place marker (pm) for beginning of rnd.

Increase Rnd: *K1, M1-u; repeat from * to end—16 sts. Purl 1 rnd. Pm after sts 4, 8, and 12.

Begin Pattern: Begin pattern from Chart A; work Rnds 1–28 once, Rnds 17–28 six times, then Rnds 17–26 once, working increases as indicated in Chart—448 sts.

Next Rnd: Change to Chart B; work Rnds 1–16 once, working increases as indicated in Chart—512 sts.

Next Rnd: Change to Garter st (knit 1 rnd, purl 1 rnd), increase 8 sts this rnd, then every other rnd 6 times, as follows, ending with a purl rnd: *Yo, knit to marker, yo, slip marker (sm); repeat from * to end—560 sts. BO all sts purlwise.

FINISHING

Carefully remove waste yarn. Thread tail through live sts, pull tight and fasten off.

Block as desired.

FINISHED MEASUREMENTS

Approximately 37 ″ square, after blocking

YARN

Peace Fleece DK Sport Weight (70% wool / 30% mohair; 350 yards / 4 ounces): 3 hanks Father's Grey

NEEDLES

▸ One set of five double-pointed needles (dpn) size US 6 (4 mm)
▸ One 32 ″ (80 cm) long circular (circ) needle size US 6 (4 mm) Change needle size if necessary to obtain correct gauge.

NOTIONS

Waste yarn; stitch markers

GAUGE

20 sts and 24 rnds = 4 ″ (10 cm) in Garter stitch, before blocking

CHART A

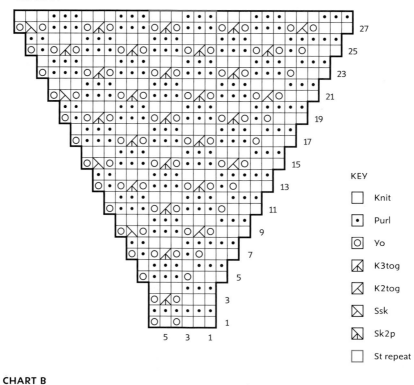

27
25
23
21
19
17
15
13
11
9
7
5
3
1

5   3   1

KEY

☐ Knit

• Purl

◉ Yo

◩ K3tog

◪ K2tog

◸ Ssk

◺ Sk2p

☐ St repeat

CHART B

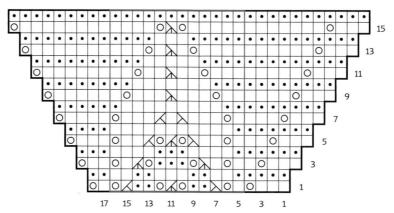

15
13
11
9
7
5
3
1

17   15   13   11   9   7   5   3   1

1965 ARM WARMERS

The French haute couture designer Yves Saint Laurent was famous for his innovative use of fabrics, and frequently combined fine textiles with highly textured knits in his collections. Such an example was a wedding dress he created in 1965, made from super bulky wool and trimmed with silk satin ribbons. The stitch pattern in the dress inspired the one I chose for these arm warmers. Both functional and stylish, they are a favorite trans-season accessory.

SIZES

Small (Medium, Large)

FINISHED MEASUREMENTS

Approximately 6 ¾ (7 ½, 8 ¼)" hand circumference

YARN

Louet Gems Sport Weight (100% merino wool; 225 yards / 100 grams): 1 (2, 2) hanks #01 Champagne

NEEDLES

One set of five double-pointed needles (dpn) size US 2 (2.75 mm) Change needle size if necessary to obtain correct gauge.

NOTIONS

Stitch marker

GAUGE

21 sts and 30 rnds = 3" (7.5 cm) in Moss Stitch

ABBREVIATIONS

RT (right twist): K2tog, but do not drop sts from left-hand needle; insert right-hand needle between 2 sts just worked and knit first st again; slip both sts from left-hand needle together.

CS (cluster stitch): Slip 5 sts purlwise wyib, dropping extra wraps; return 5 elongated sts to left-hand needle, [k5tog, but do not drop sts from left-hand needle, yo] twice, k5tog, slipping all 5 sts from left-hand needle together.

STITCH PATTERNS

Baby Cable Ribbing

(multiple of 4 sts; 2-rnd repeat)
Rnd 1: *K2, p2; repeat from * to end.
Rnd 2: *RT, p2; repeat from * to end.
Repeat Rnds 1 and 2 for Baby Cable Ribbing.

Cluster Stitch in-the-Round

(multiple of 5 sts; 4-rnd repeat)
Rnd 1: Purl.

Rnd 2: Knit.
Rnd 3: *P1, wrapping yarn 3 times; repeat from * to end.
Rnd 4: *CS; repeat from * to end.
Repeat Rnds 1–4 for Cluster Stitch in-the-Round.

Moss Stitch

(multiple of 2 sts; 4-rnd repeat)
Rnd 1: *K1, p1; repeat from * to end.
Rnds 2 and 3: *P1, k1; repeat from * to end.
Rnd 4: Repeat Rnd 1.
Repeat Rnds 1–4 for Moss Stitch.

Cluster Stitch in Rows

(multiple of 5 sts; 4-row repeat)
Row 1 (WS): Knit.
Row 2: Knit.
Row 3: *K1, wrapping yarn 3 times; repeat from * to end.
Row 4: *CS; repeat from * to end.
Repeat Rows 1–4 for Cluster Stitch in Rows.

CUFF

CO 56 (60, 64) sts. Divide sts evenly among 4 dpns. Join for working in the round, being careful not to twist sts; place marker (pm) for beginning of rnd. Begin Baby Cable Ribbing; work even for 1½".

Next Rnd: K2tog (k1, k1), knit to last st, k1 (k1, k1-f/b)—55 (60, 65) sts.

Next Rnd: Change to Cluster St in-the-Rnd; work Rnds 1–4 five times, then Rnds 1 and 2 once.

Decrease Rnd: *K3 (4, 4), k2tog; repeat from * to last 5 (0, 5) sts, knit to end—45 (50, 55) sts remain.

Next Rnd: Change to Moss St; work even until piece measures 8" from the beginning, ending with Rnd 4 of pattern. Knit 1 rnd.

HAND

Next Rnd: Change to Cluster St in-the-Rnd; work Rnds 1–4 three times.

Divide for Thumb Opening

Increase Row 1 (WS): Change to working back and forth. M1, work Cluster St in Rows across next 45 (50, 55) sts, M1—47 (52, 57) sts.

Increase Row 2: K1-f/b, work to last st, k1-f/b—49 (54, 59) sts.

Next Row: Keeping first and last 2 sts of every row in Garter st (knit every row), work even until 3 vertical repeats of Cluster St in Rows have been completed. Knit 1 row.

PALM

Join for working in the rnd; pm for beginning of rnd. K2tog, knit to last 4 (2, 4) sts, [k2tog] twice (once, twice)—46 (52, 56) sts. Change to Baby Cable Ribbing; work even for 1". BO all sts in pattern.

FINISHING

Block as desired.

CABLED BERET

In my opinion, just about everyone looks good in a beret. This archetypal topper tends to suit all styles and facial characteristics. Wear it neat and trim or with a bohemian slouch—either way, it is always *au courant*.

BERET

Using circ needle, CO 108 sts. Join for working in the rnd, being careful not to twist sts; place marker (pm) for beginning of rnd. Begin Garter st (purl 1 rnd, knit 1 rnd); work even for 5 rnds.

Shape Brim: *K1-f/b; repeat from * to end—216 sts.

Next Rnd: Change to Cable Pattern from Chart; work even until piece measures 5″ from the beginning.

Next Rnd: [Work 36 sts, pm] 5 times, work to end.

Shape Crown
Note: Change to dpns when necessary for number of sts on needle.

Decrease Rnd 1: Decrease 12 sts this rnd, then every other rnd 14 times, as follows: *Work 2 sts, ssp, work to 2 sts before next marker, p2tog; repeat from * to end—36 sts remain.

Decrease Rnd 2: *Work 3 sts, p3tog; repeat from * to end—24 sts remain.

Decrease Rnd 3: *Work 2 sts, p2tog; repeat from * to end—18 sts remain.

Decrease Rnd 4: *K1, k2tog; repeat from * to end—12 sts remain. Transfer remaining sts to single dpn, removing markers.

Next Rnd: *K2tog; repeat from * to end—6 sts remain. Work I-Cord (see Special Techniques, page 122) on remaining sts for ½″. Cut yarn, leaving 8″ tail. Thread tail through remaining sts, pull tight and fasten off.

Block as desired.

FINISHED MEASUREMENTS

23 ¼ ″ circumference

YARN

St-Denis Nordique (100% wool; 150 yards / 50 grams): 1 ball #5895 Fjord

NEEDLES

▶ One 16 ″ (40 cm) long circular (circ) needle size US 2 (2.75 mm)
▶ One set of five double-pointed needles (dpn) size US 2 (2.75 mm) Change needle size if necessary to obtain correct gauge.

NOTIONS

Stitch markers (one in contrasting color for beginning of rnd); cable needle (cn)

GAUGE

27 sts and 39 rnds = 4 ″ (10 cm) in Cable Pattern from Chart

CABLE PATTERN

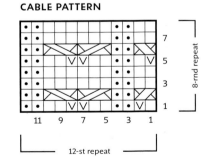

8-rnd repeat

12-st repeat

KEY

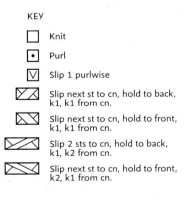

☐ Knit

• Purl

V Slip 1 purlwise

Slip next st to cn, hold to back, k1, k1 from cn.

Slip next st to cn, hold to front, k1, k1 from cn.

Slip 2 sts to cn, hold to back, k1, k2 from cn.

Slip next st to cn, hold to front, k2, k1 from cn.

MODERN PILLOW

If you are new to colorwork and steeks, this is an ideal, small project to practice both techniques. The front of this pillowcase is knitted as a tube using only two colors. One yarn is tweedy while the other has a fine halo of angora, causing the textures and graphic elements to truly pop. Once the pillow front is completed, a steek is cut into the tube in order to make a flat panel, and stitches are picked up to create the single-color backside. The result is a sophisticated accessory for the home.

NOTES
Steek sts are worked in Stranded (Fair Isle) Colorwork Method (see Special Techniques, page 122) and may be worked as vertical stripes or in a checkerboard pattern, as written, if preferred.

FRONT
Using MC, CO 118 sts. Join for working in the rnd, being careful not to twist sts; place marker (pm) for beginning of rnd.

Begin Pattern: Work Fair Isle Pattern from Chart to last 9 sts, pm, work to end, alternating colors every stitch to create striped steek (See Notes, above, and Special Techniques, page 122).

FAIR ISLE PATTERN

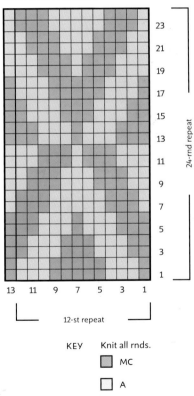

24-rnd repeat

23
21
19
17
15
13
11
9
7
5
3
1

13 11 9 7 5 3 1

12-st repeat

KEY   Knit all rnds.
        ■ MC
        □ A

FINISHED MEASUREMENTS
▸ Approximately 15 " square, before inserting pillow form
▸ Approximately 16 " square, with pillow form

YARN
▸ Briggs & Little Sport (100% wool; 430 yards / 4 ounces): 2 hanks #11 Dark Grey (MC)
▸ Classic Elite Yarns Fresco (60% wool / 30% baby alpaca / 10% angora; 164 yards / 50 grams): 2 hanks #5336 Oatmeal (A)

NEEDLES
One 16 " (40 cm) long circular (circ) needle size US 5 (3.75 mm)
Change needle size if necessary to obtain correct gauge.

NOTIONS
Stitch markers (one in contrasting color for beginning of rnd); sewing machine or sewing needle and matching thread; five 7/8 " buttons; 16 " square pillow form

GAUGE
29 sts and 28 rnds = 4 " (10 cm) in Fair Isle Pattern from Chart

Work even until 4 vertical repeats of Chart have been completed, then work Rnds 1–12 once (piece should measure approximately 15″ from the beginning). BO all sts. Cut pillow open down center of steek. Secure pillow edges by machine or hand sewing down the center of each steek edge st.

TOP BACK PANEL

With RS of Front facing, using MC and working along BO edge, pick up and knit 1 st from last steek st before Chart sts, 108 sts from Chart sts, and 1 st from first steek st after Chart sts— 110 sts. Begin St st, beginning with a purl row; work even for 48 rows.

Decrease Row (RS): *K4, k2tog, k5; repeat from * to end—100 sts remain. Knit 7 rows.

Buttonhole Row: K10, [BO 4 sts, k15] 4 times, BO 4, k10. Continuing in Garter st (knit every row), work even for 6 rows, CO 4 sts over BO sts on first row. BO all sts knitwise.

BOTTOM BACK PANEL

Work as for Top Back Panel, picking up sts from CO edge, and omitting buttonholes.

FINISHING

Sew side seams, overlapping Back Panels so that Garter st section of Bottom Back Panel is behind Garter st section of Top Back Panel. Sew buttons opposite buttonholes.

Block as desired.

ARROWHEAD KNEESOCKS

Kneesocks aren't just for prep school girls, as these elegant, lacy stockings prove. The arrowhead lace pattern couldn't be easier, and shaped Stockinette-stitch panels on each side of the calf ensure a snug fit. The result is a stunning twist on classic hosiery.

STITCH PATTERN

Twisted Rib
(multiple of 2 sts; 1-rnd repeat)
All Rnds: *K1-tbl, p1-tbl; repeat from * to end.

LEG

CO 80 sts. Distribute sts among 4 needles (15-25-15-25). Join for working in the rnd, being careful not to twist sts; place marker (pm) for beginning of rnd. Begin Twisted Rib; work even for 1 ¼". Purl 2 rnds. Knit 1 rnd.

Begin Pattern: [Work Arrowhead Lace from Chart across next 30 sts, k10] twice. Work even until Leg measures 2 ½" from the beginning.

Shape Leg: Decrease 2 sts this rnd, every 20 rnds 3 times, then every 10 rnds 4 times, as follows: *Needles 1 and 2:* Work 30 sts, k2tog, knit to end of Needle 2; *Needles 3 and 4:* Work to last 2 sts on Needle 4, ssk—64 sts remain. Work even until piece measures 14" from the beginning, ending with Rnd 2 or 4. Slip last st from Needle 4 to Needle 1, and last st from Needle 2 to Needle 3 (16-16-16-16).

SIZES

To fit women's shoe sizes 6–10

FINISHED MEASUREMENTS

▶ 8 " Foot circumference
▶ 10 " calf circumference
▶ 15 ½" Leg length to base of Heel
▶ 8 ½" Foot length from back of Heel

YARN

Fortissima Socka (75% superwash wool / 25% nylon; 231 yards / 50 grams): 3 skeins #1002 Black

NEEDLES

One set of five double-pointed needles (dpn) size US 0 (2 mm) Change needle size if necessary to obtain correct gauge.

NOTIONS

Stitch marker

GAUGE

▶ 34 sts and 46 rnds = 4 " (10 cm) in Stockinette stitch (St st)
▶ 30 sts and 48 rnds = 4 " (10 cm) in Arrowhead Lace from Chart

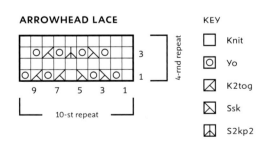

ARROWHEAD LACE

4-rnd repeat

10-st repeat

KEY

☐ Knit

◯ Yo

⧄ K2tog

⧅ Ssk

△ S2kp2

HEEL FLAP

Slip sts from Needle 2 to Needle 1, removing marker. Leave remaining 32 sts on 2 needles for instep. Work back and forth on Needles 1 and 2 only.

Set-Up Row 1 (RS): Slip 1, knit to end.

Set-Up Row 2: Slip 1, purl to end.

Row 1 (RS): *Slip 1, k1; repeat from * to end.

Row 2: Slip 1, purl to end.

Repeat Rows 1 and 2 twelve times.

Turn Heel

Set-Up Row 1: Slip 1, k17, k2tog-tbl, k1, turn.

Set-Up Row 2: Slip 1, p5, p2tog, p1, turn.

Row 1: Slip 1, knit to 1 st before gap, k2tog-tbl (the 2 sts on either side of gap), k1, turn.

Row 2: Slip 1, purl to 1 st before gap, p2tog (the 2 sts on either side of gap), p1, turn.

Repeat Rows 1 and 2 five times, omitting the final k1 and p1 sts in the last repeat of Rows 1 and 2—18 sts remain.

Gusset

Next Row (RS): *Needle 1:* Slip 1, knit across Heel Flap sts, pick up and knit 14 sts along left side of Heel Flap, pick up and knit 1 st from row below first st on Needle 2; *Needles 2 and 3:* Continue Arrowhead Lace from Chart as established; *Needle 4:* Pick up and knit 1 st from row below first Heel Flap st, pick up and knit 14 sts along left side of Heel Flap, k9 from Needle 1. Join for working in the rnd; pm for beginning of rnd—80 sts (24-16-16-24).

Decrease Rnd: *Needle 1:* Knit to last 2 sts, k2tog; *Needles 2 and 3:* Work even as established; *Needle 4:* Ssk, knit to end—78 sts remain. Work even for 1 rnd.

Repeat Decrease Rnd every other rnd 7 times—64 sts remain (16-16-16-16).

FOOT

Work even until Foot measures 2″ less than desired length from back of Heel. Knit 4 rnds.

TOE

Decrease Rnd: *Needle 1:* Knit to last 3 sts, k2tog k1; *Needle 2:* K1, ssk, knit to end; *Needle 3:* Knit to last 3 sts, k2tog, k1; *Needle 4:* K1, ssk, knit to end—60 sts remain. Knit 1 rnd.

Repeat Decrease Rnd every other rnd 7 times, then every rnd 4 times—16 sts remain. Knit to end of Needle 1.

FINISHING

Break yarn, leaving long tail. Transfer sts from Needle 1 to Needle 4, and sts from Needle 3 to Needle 2. Using Kitchener st (see Special Techniques, page 122), graft Toe sts.

Block as desired.

SNEAK IN A FEW ROWS

—during lunch break

—before meeting

—while kids nap

—during movie

—waiting for water to boil

—during kids' playdate

—waiting for school bus

—during recital

—waiting for pizza to arrive

—between ice cream and bedtime

p.m.

SPIRAL TWEED CLOCHE

This hat is a perfect accent to just about any casual outfit—it's feminine but not fussy, provides a great cover for unkempt hair, and the hand-dyed yarn goes with anything. It is worked up to the crown as a simple tube with spiraling purl stitches. The cloche shape is created by sewing a grosgrain ribbon about two inches above the brim; this causes the body of the hat to hug and the brim to flare. An optional brooch or megabutton (shown here) adds some extra personality.

NOTES

For optimal fit, choose a size about 1" larger than actual head circumference. A grosgrain ribbon sewn inside the hat once it's completed will make it conform to the actual head circumference as well as create the brim.

BRIM

Using larger needles, CO 84 (90, 96) sts. Join for working in the rnd, being careful not to twist sts; place marker (pm) for beginning of rnd. Purl 1 rnd. Knit 1 rnd. Change to Diagonal Rib Pattern from Chart; working Rnds 1–6 only, work even until piece measures 1 ¾" from the beginning.

SIZES

Small (Medium, Large)

FINISHED MEASUREMENTS

18 ¾ (20, 21 ¼)" circumference

YARN

Manos del Uruguay Wool Clásica Space Dyed (100% wool; 138 yards / 100 grams): 1 hank #108 Granite

NEEDLES

▶ One set of five double-pointed needles (dpn) size US 8 (5 mm)
▶ One set of five double-pointed needles size US 7 (4.5 mm)
Change needle size if necessary to obtain correct gauge.

NOTIONS

Stitch marker; sewing needle and matching thread; ¾ yard 1"-wide grosgrain ribbon; brooch or large button (optional)

GAUGE

18 sts and 24 rnds = 4" (10 cm) in Diagonal Rib Pattern from Chart, using larger needles

DIAGONAL RIB PATTERN

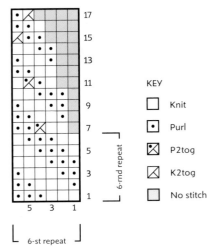

KEY

☐ Knit
▪ Purl
⊠ P2tog
⊠ K2tog
▨ No stitch

6-rnd repeat

6-st repeat

Change to smaller needles. Work even until piece measures 5 (5 ½, 6)" from the beginning, ending with Rnd 6 of Chart.

Shape Crown: Work Rnds 7–17 of Chart once, working decreases as indicated in Chart—28 (30, 32) sts remain. Work even for 1 rnd.

Next Rnd: *P2tog; repeat from * to end—14 (15, 16) sts remain.

Next Rnd: P0 (1, 0), *p2tog; repeat from * to end—7 (8, 8) sts remain. Cut yarn, leaving a 12" tail. Thread tail through remaining sts twice, pull tight and fasten off.

FINISHING

Cut a 19 ¾ (21, 22 ¼)" length of grosgrain ribbon. Overlap ends of ribbon by 1" and pin inside Cloche, about 2" from CO edge. Using sewing needle and thread, sew in place. *Note: Circumference of ribbon is slightly smaller than circumference of Cloche; ease in slightly as you sew ribbon in.*

Block as desired.

Sew button or attach brooch on side of hat, if desired.

Spaghetti w/ tuna IN...
olive; Red wine sauce
Chicken PROVINCIALE
w/ Leeks
tomato
w/ Shiitake
mushroom

LEAFY KNOT CLUTCH

This little clutch is perfect for carrying the essentials—wallet, keys, cell phone, and lip gloss—when heading out for a night on the town. Or it could be used as a bag for a special, small gift. The straps are intentionally different, with one just long enough to slip over the other in order to secure the bag, and the other sized to slip over the wrist. The base is worked in sturdy Garter stitch; the body is worked in a pretty, lacy leaf pattern.

BASE
CO 3 sts. Knit 1 row.

Shape Base
Row 1 (RS): [K1, yo] twice, k1—5 sts.

Row 2: [K1, k1-tbl] twice, k1.

Row 3: K2, yo, knit to last 2 sts, yo, k2—7 sts.

Row 4: K2, k1-tbl, knit to last 3 sts, k1-tbl, k2.

Repeat Rows 3 and 4 fifteen times—37 sts. Knit 4 rows.

Decrease Row: Decrease 2 sts this row, then every other row 16 times, as follows: K1, ssk, knit to last 3 sts, k2tog, k1—3 sts remain. Knit 1 row. BO all sts.

FINISHED MEASUREMENTS
▸ 15 " circumference
▸ 8 " long, not including handles

YARN
Nashua Handknits Creative Focus Cotton DK (100% Egyptian mercerized cotton; 118 yards / 50 grams): 2 balls #0210 Dark Navy

NEEDLES
One set of five double-pointed needles (dpn) size US 4 (3.5 mm) Change needle size if necessary to obtain correct gauge.

NOTIONS
Crochet hook size US E/4 (3.5 mm); stitch markers (one in contrasting color for beginning of rnd); stitch holders

GAUGE
24 sts and 32 rnds = 4 " (10 cm) in Leafy Knot Pattern from Chart

LEAFY KNOT PATTERN

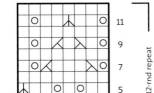

12-rnd repeat

8-st repeat

KEY

☐ Knit

⧀ Yo

⧄ K2tog

⧅ Ssk

⧄ S2kp2

Ⅴ This is worked at end of rnd only: Remove marker, slip 1 from next rnd, replace marker for new beginning of rnd.

BAG

With RS of Base facing, pick up (but do not knit) each Garter st bump around outside edge—72 sts. Join for working in the rnd; place marker (pm) for beginning of rnd. Purl 1 rnd, knit 1 rnd.

Next Rnd: *K3, M1; repeat from * to end—96 sts.

Begin Pattern: Begin Leafy Knot Pattern from Chart; work Rnds 1–12 three times, then Rnds 1–6 once, ending 2 sts before end of last rnd. Place last 69 sts worked on holder, removing marker.

Shape First Half of Long Handle: Working back and forth on remaining 27 sts, and continuing in Leafy Knot Pattern, decrease 1 st at end of this row, then every other row 11 times—15 sts remain. *Note: When working Rows 7, 9, and 11 of Chart, omit yo before first st and after last st worked. Do not work a yo in st pattern without a corresponding decrease. Do not work a decrease (except when shaping side edge) without a corresponding yo.* Work even until handle measures 4", ending with a WS row. Place sts on holder.

Shape First Half of Short Handle: With RS facing, transfer next 24 sts to needle. With tip of left-hand needle, pick up (but do not knit) 3 sts directly to the right of first st—27 sts. Rejoin yarn. Continuing in Leafy Knot Pattern, decrease 1 st at beginning of this row, then every other row 11 times—15 sts remain. Work even for 1 row. Place sts on holder.

Shape Second Half of Short Handle: With RS facing, transfer next 24 sts to needle. With tip of left-hand needle, pick up (but do not knit) 3 sts directly to the right of first st—27 sts. Rejoin yarn. Continuing in Leafy Knot Pattern, decrease 1 st at end of this row, then every other row 11 times—15 sts remain. Work even for 1 row. Place sts on holder.

Shape Second Half of Long Handle: With RS facing, pick up (but do not knit) 3 sts to the left of sts on holder. Transfer next 21 sts to needle. With tip of left-hand needle, pick up (but do not knit) 3 sts directly to the right of first st—27 sts. Rejoin yarn. Continuing in Leafy Knot Pattern, decrease 1 st at beginning of this row, then every other row 11 times—15 sts remain. Work even until handle measures 4", ending with a WS row. Place sts on holder.

FINISHING

Using Three-Needle BO (see Special Techniques, page 122), join halves of handles together. Work 1 rnd of single crochet around all edges.

Block as desired.

FIR CONE SHRUG

This shrug is one of the most versatile pieces in this collection. You can wear it to work with a collared shirt just as easily as you can put it on over your pajamas for an evening of cozy comfort. It begins as a long strip that is connected at the ends of the arms, where live stitches are sewn together with the wrong sides facing to produce a decorative seam on the outside. Increases and decreases along the edges make for a pretty, wavy border.

NOTES

Charts B and C will be worked when shaping each side of the armhole. Make note of the row number of Chart A that you end on before beginning the armhole. You will begin on the next row of Chart B or C, depending on which side of the armhole you are shaping.

CENTER BACK PANEL

Using circ needle, CO 21 sts. Knit 1 row.

Begin Chart (RS): Begin Fir Cone Pattern from Chart A; work even until piece measures approximately 32 ¼ (35, 37 ½)" from the beginning, ending with Row 5. BO all sts.

LEFT BACK/FRONT

With RS facing and BO edge of Center Back Panel at right, pick up and knit 121 (131, 141) sts along Center Back Panel. Knit 1 WS row.

Begin Chart (RS): Begin Fir Cone Pattern from Chart A; work even until piece measures approximately 10 (10 ¾, 11 ½)" from the beginning, ending with a WS row.

Begin Armhole (RS): Work across next 61 (66, 71) sts. Place remaining 60 (65, 70) sts on st holder. Purl 1 row. Make note of last row worked in Chart A.

Note: When working the following armhole decreases, work only as many rows of the chart as you need to decrease the number of sts required. If your final decrease row requires you to work an sk2p decrease, and you only need to decrease 1 st instead of 2, work ssk instead of sk2p.

SIZES

To fit bust sizes 32–36 (38–42, 44–48)"

FINISHED MEASUREMENTS

▸ 68 (72, 77)" around center opening

▸ 34 (36, 38 ½)" armhole to armhole

YARN

Kraemer Yarns Mauch Chunky (60% New Zealand wool / 40% domestic wool; 120 yards / 100 grams): 6 (7, 8) skeins #1032 Bing Cherry

NEEDLES

▸ One 32" (80 cm) long circular (circ) needle size US 8 (5 mm)

▸ One straight needle size US 8 (5 mm)

Change needle size if necessary to obtain correct gauge.

NOTIONS

Crochet hook size US H/8 (5 mm); stitch holders

GAUGE

15 sts and 21 rows = 4" (10 cm) in Fir Cone Pattern from Chart A

CHART A: FIR CONE PATTERN

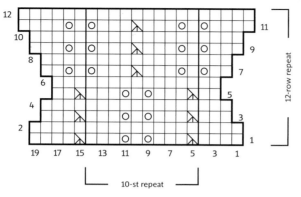

12-row repeat

10-st repeat

CHART B: ARMHOLE DECREASES, RIGHT SIDE

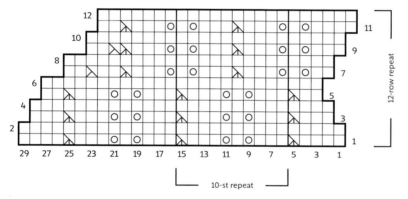

12-row repeat

10-st repeat

CHART C: ARMHOLE DECREASES, LEFT SIDE

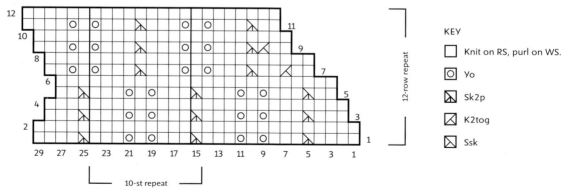

12-row repeat

10-st repeat

KEY

☐	Knit on RS, purl on WS.
⊙	Yo
⊠	Sk2p
◩	K2tog
◪	Ssk

Shape Right Edge of Armhole (RS): Work decreases as indicated in Chart B, beginning with row after last row worked in Chart A, decreasing a total of 12 (13, 14) sts, and ending with a WS row—49 (53, 57) sts remain. Cut yarn, leaving a 48″ tail. Place sts on st holder.

Shape Left Edge of Armhole (RS): With RS facing, rejoin yarn to sts on holder. With tip of right-hand needle, pick up 1 st in last st of previously worked section, work to end—61 (66, 71) sts. Purl 1 row.

Next Row (RS): Work decreases as indicated in Chart C, beginning with row after last row worked in Chart A, decreasing a total of 12 (13, 14) sts, and ending with a WS row—49 (53, 57) sts remain. Cut yarn.

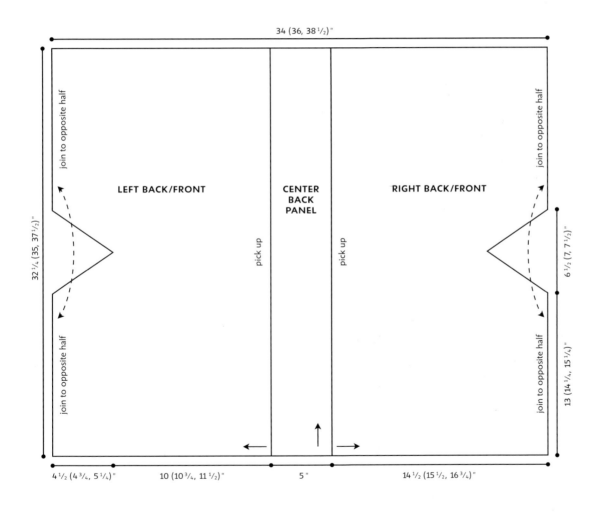

Transfer sts from st holder to straight needle. With WSs together, using Three-Needle BO (see Special Techniques, page 122), join sides. *Note: Three-Needle BO is usually worked with RSs together; here, it is worked with WSs together to create a decorative seam on the RS.*

RIGHT BACK/FRONT

With RS facing and CO edge of Center Back Panel at right, pick up and knit 121 (131, 141) sts along Center Back Panel. Complete as for Left Back/Front.

FINISHING

With RS facing, using crochet hook, work 2 rnds of single crochet around all edges, including armholes. Fasten off.

Block as desired.

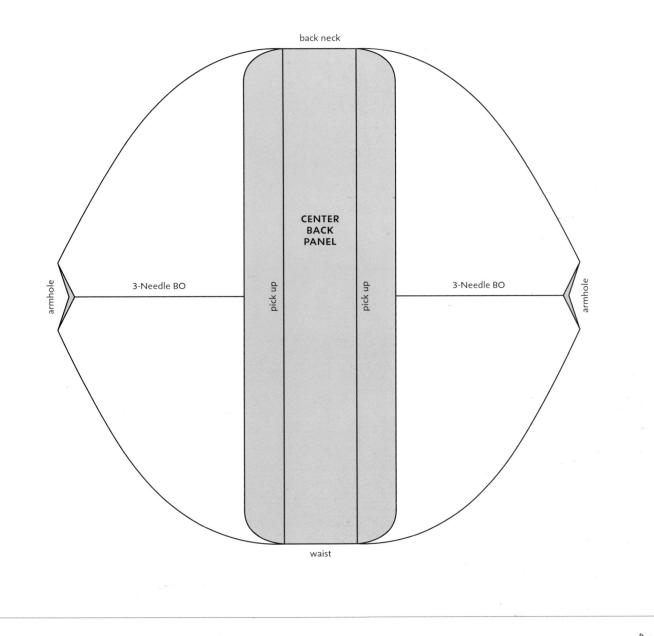

SHALLOTS
$11.00/
#

ELEMENTAL PULLOVER

At once minimal and elegant, seamless yoked sweaters are the ultimate knitted garment; no other sweater style is quite as simple, versatile, and distinctly feminine. Made from a delicious alpaca and wool yarn, this is a soothing project that is as much a treat to wear as it is to create.

BODY

With circ needle, CO 216 (240, 264, 288, 312, 336) sts. Join for working in the rnd, being careful not to twist sts; place marker (pm) for beginning of rnd. Begin St st (knit every rnd); work even for 6 rnds. Purl 1 rnd (turning rnd). Continuing in St st; work even until piece measures 15 (15, 15 ¼, 15 ¾, 16, 16 ¼)" from the beginning.

Divide for Front and Back (RS): K4 (5, 5, 6, 6, 7), place last 8 (10, 10, 12, 12, 14) sts worked on holder for left underarm, removing marker, k108 (120, 132, 144, 156, 168), place last 8 (10, 10, 12, 12, 14) sts worked on holder for right underarm, knit to end—100 (110, 122, 132, 144, 154) sts remain for Front and Back. Set aside, but do not cut yarn.

SLEEVES

With dpn, CO 56 (60, 64, 68, 72, 76) sts. Join for working in the rnd, being careful not to twist sts; pm for beginning of rnd. Begin St st; work even for 6 rnds. Purl 1 rnd (turning rnd). Continuing in St st, work even until piece measures 7 ¾ (6 ½, 6 ¾, 5 ¼, 5 ½, 4 ¼)" from the beginning.

Shape Sleeve: Increase 2 sts this rnd, every 14 rnds 5 (5, 3, 3, 1, 1) time(s), then every 8 rnds 2 (4, 8, 10, 14, 16) times, as follows: K1, M1-r, work to last st, M1-l, k1—72 (80, 88, 96, 104, 112) sts. Work even until piece measures 19 ½ (19 ¾, 20 ½, 21, 21 ½, 22)" from turning rnd.

Next Rnd: K4 (5, 5, 6, 6, 7), place last 8 (10, 10, 12, 12, 14) sts worked on holder for left underarm, removing marker, knit to end—64 (70, 78, 84, 92, 98) sts remain. Cut yarn and set aside.

YOKE

Using yarn attached to Body, knit across 64 (70, 78, 84, 92, 98) sts for left Sleeve, pm for left Front raglan, knit across 100 (110, 122, 132, 144, 154) sts for Front, pm for right Front raglan, knit across 64 (70, 78, 84, 92, 98) sts for right Sleeve, pm for right Back raglan, knit across 100 (110, 122, 132, 144, 154) sts for Back, pm for left Back raglan and beginning of rnd—328 (360, 400, 432, 472, 504) sts. Knit 1 rnd.

SIZES

X-Small (Small, Medium, Large, 1X-Large, 2X-Large)

FINISHED MEASUREMENTS

30 ¾ (34 ¼, 37 ¾, 41 ¼, 44 ½, 48)" bust

YARN

Berroco Ultra Alpaca Light (50% superfine alpaca / 50% Peruvian highland wool; 144 yards / 50 grams): 9 (10, 11, 13, 14, 16) hanks #4201 Winter White

NEEDLES

▸ One 24" (60 cm) long or longer circular (circ) needle size US 4 (3.5 mm)
▸ One set of five double-pointed needles (dpn) size US 4 (3.5 mm) Change needle size if necessary to obtain correct gauge.

NOTIONS

Stitch markers (one in contrasting color for beginning of rnd); stitch holders

GAUGE

28 sts and 36 rnds = 4" (10 cm) in Stockinette stitch (St st)

Shape Yoke

Decrease Rnd 1: Decrease 8 sts this rnd, then every other rnd 4 (4, 5, 5, 6, 6) times, as follows: *K1, k2tog, knit to 3 sts before next marker, ssk, k1; repeat from * 3 times—288 (320, 352, 384, 416, 448) sts remain. Work even until yoke measures 2 (1 ½, 1 ¾, 3 ¼, 3, 3)″, removing all markers except for beginning of rnd marker.

Next Rnd: *K18 (20, 22, 24, 26, 28), pm; repeat from * to end.

Decrease Rnd 2: Decrease 16 sts this rnd, then every 4 (4, 4, 3, 3, 3) rnds 11 (13, 14, 16, 18, 20) times, as follows: *Knit to 2 sts before marker, k2tog; repeat from * to end—96 (96, 112, 112, 112, 112) sts remain.

Sizes Medium and Large Only

Decrease Rnd 3: Knit to 2 sts before marker, k2tog, [knit through next marker to 2 sts before following marker, k2tog] 7 times, knit to end—104 sts remain.

All Sizes

Work even for 4″. Change to Garter st (purl 1 rnd, knit 1 rnd); work even for 10 rnds. BO all sts.

FINISHING

Using Kitchener st (see Special Techniques, page 122), graft underarm sts. Turn Body and Sleeve hems to WS at turning rnd and sew to WS, being careful not to let sts show on RS.

Block as desired.

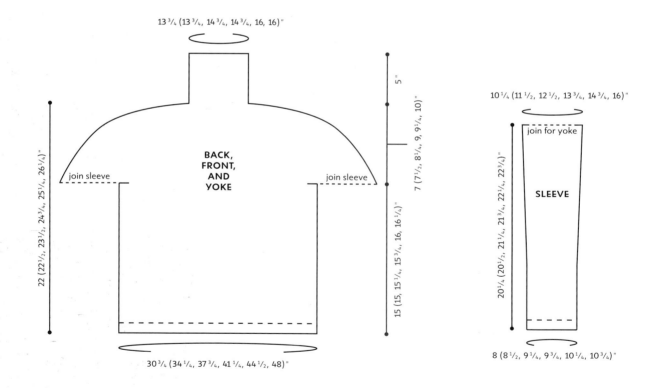

13 ¾ (13 ¾, 14 ¾, 14 ¾, 16, 16)″

5″

7 (7½, 8¼, 9, 9¼, 10)″

22 (22½, 23½, 24¾, 25¾, 26¼)″

join sleeve

BACK, FRONT, AND YOKE

join sleeve

15 (15, 15¼, 15¾, 16, 16¼)″

30¾ (34¼, 37¾, 41¼, 44½, 48)″

10¼ (11½, 12½, 13¾, 14¾, 16)″

join for yoke

SLEEVE

20¼ (20½, 21¼, 21¾, 22¼, 22¾)″

8 (8½, 9¼, 9¾, 10¼, 10¾)″

LINEN MARKET BAG

While this bag is made from just two balls of linen, it is big enough to carry a substantial farmer's market haul. Keep one with you all the time so you're always ready for spontaneous shopping. As much as three times stronger than cotton (and with a lovely natural sheen), linen is an ideal fiber for such heavy-duty use.

STITCH PATTERN

Diagonal Mesh

(multiple of 4 sts; 6-rnd repeat)

Rnd 1: *Yo, sk2p, yo, k1; repeat from * to end.

Rnds 2 and 4: Knit.

Rnd 3: *K1, yo, sk2p, yo; repeat from * to end.

Rnd 5: Remove marker, k1, reposition marker for new beginning of rnd, *k1, yo, sk2p, yo; repeat from * to end.

Rnd 6: Knit.

Repeat Rnds 5 and 6 for Diagonal Mesh.

BASE

CO 12 sts. Divide sts evenly among 4 needles. Join for working in the rnd, being careful not to twist sts; place marker (pm) for beginning of rnd. Purl 1 rnd.

Shape Base

Rnd 1: [K1, yo, knit to end of needle] 4 times—16 sts.

Rnd 2: Purl.

Repeat Rnds 1 and 2 twenty-one times—100 sts. *Note: Change to circ needle when appropriate for number of sts on needles.*

BODY

Begin Pattern: Change to Diagonal Mesh; work Rnds 1–4 once, then work Rnds 5 and 6 until piece measures 10″ from beginning of Body, ending with Rnd 6. Change to Garter st (purl 1 rnd, knit 1 rnd); work even for 1¼″, ending with a purl rnd.

FINISHED MEASUREMENTS

▶ Approximately 11 ¼ " long, not including Handles

▶ 22 ¼ " circumference

YARN

Drops Lin (100% linen; 131 yards / 50 grams): 2 skeins #106 Dark Lilac

NEEDLES

▶ One set of five double-pointed needles (dpn) size US 5 (3.75 mm)

▶ One 16 " (40 cm) long circular (circ) needle size US 5 (3.75 mm) Change needle size if necessary to obtain correct gauge.

NOTIONS

Stitch marker; stitch holders

GAUGE

18 sts and 36 rnds = 4 " (10 cm) in Garter stitch

DIAGONAL MESH PATTERN

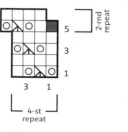

5

3

1

2-rnd repeat

3   1

4-st repeat

KEY

☐ Knit

⊡ Yo

⊠ Sk2p

▨ This is worked at beginning of rnd only: Remove marker, k1, reposition marker for new beginning of rnd.

HANDLES

First Strap

K25, transfer remaining 75 sts to holder.

Shape Strap

Row 1: Knit.

Row 2: K2, k2tog, knit to last 4 sts, ssk, k2—23 sts remain.

Repeat Rows 1 and 2 seven times— 9 sts remain. Continuing in Garter st, work even until Strap measures 8 ¾" from beginning of shaping. Place sts on holder.

Second, Third, and Fourth Straps:
Transfer next 25 sts to needle. Work as for First Strap.

FINISHING

Using Kitchener st (see Special Techniques, page 122), graft Straps together. Thread CO tail through CO sts, pull tight and fasten off.

Block as desired.

SMOCKED LACE SCARF

I have a minimal aesthetic when it comes to jewelry and tend to avoid any pieces that rattle or could get snagged on my clothing. Instead, I prefer to dress up an outfit with an elegant, silk-blend lace scarf, which makes a statement as grand as a piece of jewelry but without the clanking of metal.

FIRST HALF

CO 85 sts. Knit 4 rows. Begin Smocked Lace Pattern from Chart; work even until piece measures 9″ from the beginning, ending with Row 12 of pattern. Change to Sawtooth Lace Pattern from Chart; work even until piece measures 30″ from the beginning, ending with a WS row. Transfer sts to holder.

SECOND HALF

Work as for First Half. Leave sts on needle.

FINISHING

Transfer sts from st holder to second needle. With WSs together, using Three-Needle BO (see Special Techniques, page 122), join Halves. *Note: Three-Needle BO is usually worked with RSs together; here, it is worked with WSs together to create a decorative seam on the RS.*

Block as desired.

FINISHED MEASUREMENTS

Approximately 9 ½″ wide x 60″ long, after blocking

YARN

Fiddlesticks Knitting Exquisite (50% merino wool / 50% mulberry silk; 547 yards / 50 grams): 2 balls Damson

NEEDLES

One pair straight needles size US 2 (2.75 mm)
Change needle size if necessary to obtain correct gauge.

NOTIONS

Stitch holder

GAUGE

36 sts and 39 rows = 4″ (10 cm) in Sawtooth Lace Pattern from Chart, after blocking

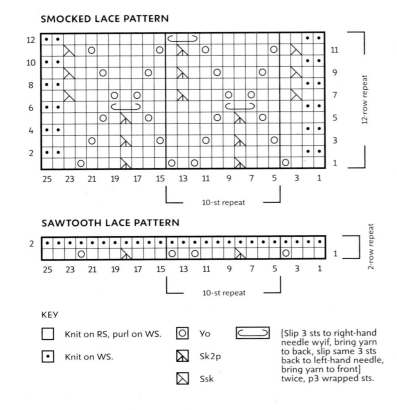

SMOCKED LACE PATTERN

SAWTOOTH LACE PATTERN

KEY

	Knit on RS, purl on WS.
	Knit on WS.
O	Yo
	Sk2p
	Ssk
	[Slip 3 sts to right-hand needle wyif, bring yarn to back, slip same 3 sts back to left-hand needle, bring yarn to front] twice, p3 wrapped sts.

PINSTRIPE SLOUCH HAT

This hat can be worn with either side facing out—the smoothness of the Stockinette-stitch side imparts a beautiful sheen, while the Reverse Stockinette-stitch side is more rustic, with an impressionistic blending of colors divided by columns of slipped stitches. The silk-wool yarn has an interesting look because of the way the silk ply coils its way around the wool core. The result is a matte yarn with flashes of luminosity.

ABBREVIATION

K1b: Knit into st below next st on left-hand needle.

STITCH PATTERN

Slipped Stitch Pattern

(multiple of 12 sts; 2-rnd repeat)

Rnd 1: *K1, p11; repeat from * to end.

Rnd 2: *K1b, p11; repeat from * to end.

Repeat Rnds 1 and 2 for Slipped Stitch Pattern.

BRIM

Using circ needle, CO 132 (144, 156) sts. Join for working in the rnd, being careful not to twist sts; place marker (pm) for beginning of rnd. Begin Garter st (purl 1 rnd, knit 1 rnd); work even for 18 rnds. Change to Slipped Stitch Pattern; work even until piece measures 6 (6 ½, 7)" from the beginning, ending with Rnd 1 of Slipped Stitch Pattern.

Shape Crown

Decrease Rnd 1: *K1b, ssp, p7, p2tog; repeat from * to end—110 (120, 130) sts remain. Work even for 5 rnds.

Decrease Rnd 2: *K1b, ssp, p5, p2tog; repeat from * to end—88 (96, 104) sts remain. Work even for 5 rnds.

Decrease Rnd 3: *K1b, ssp, p3, p2tog; repeat from * to end—66 (72, 78) sts remain. Work even for 5 rnds.

Decrease Rnd 4: *K1b, ssp, p1, p2tog; repeat from * to end—44 (48, 52) sts remain. Work even for 1 rnd.

Decrease Rnd 5: *K1b, p3tog; repeat from * to end—22 (24, 26) sts remain. Work even for 1 rnd.

FINISHING

Cut yarn, leaving a 12" tail; thread tail through remaining sts twice, pull tight and fasten off.

Block as desired.

SIZES

Small (Medium, Large)

FINISHED MEASUREMENTS

18 ¾ (20 ½, 22 ¼)" circumference

YARN

Hand Maiden Fine Yarn Silk Twist (65% wool / 35% silk; 437 yards / 100 grams): 1 hank Paris

NEEDLES

▶ One 16" (40 cm) long circular (circ) needle size US 2 (2.75 mm)
▶ One set of five double-pointed needles (dpn) size US 2 (2.75 mm)
Change needle size if necessary to obtain correct gauge.

NOTIONS

Stitch marker

GAUGE

28 sts and 36 rnds = 4" (10 cm) in Stockinette stitch (St st)

OSTRICH PLUMES STOLE

While complex in appearance, the ostrich plumes stitch pattern is actually quite simple, comprised of only two rows that are repeated four times each. Scallops form on all four sides, but a very loose cast-on is necessary in order for the stole's ends to be flexible enough to show off this feature. The stole shown here is blocked to its full dimensions, but it can also be left unblocked and worn as a scarf. When unblocked, the ostrich plumes pattern forms peaks and valleys in the knitted fabric, not unlike a freshly untied shibori scarf.

NOTES

While it isn't essential, casting on using a provisional cast-on method allows both the cast-on and bound-off edges to be finished at the same time so you can adjust the tension and make sure the edges match. I recommend using a Stem Stitch Bind-Off, which gives added control over the tension and ensures that the edges will be as loose as possible.

STOLE

Using waste yarn and provisional CO of your choice, CO 107 sts. Change to working yarn, leaving a 72″ tail. Knit 1 row. Begin Ostrich Plumes Pattern from Chart. Work even until piece measures approximately 60″ from the beginning, ending with Row 8 of Chart. Cut yarn, leaving a 72″ tail. Using Stem Stitch BO (see Special Techniques, page 122), BO all sts.

FINISHING

Carefully unpick provisional CO and place sts on spare needle. BO all sts as for opposite end.

Block as desired.

FINISHED MEASUREMENTS

Approximately 15″ wide x 56″ long, after blocking

YARN

Hand Maiden Fine Yarn Silk Twist (65% wool / 35% silk; 437 yards / 100 grams): 2 hanks Deep Plum

NEEDLES

One pair straight needles size US 5 (3.75 mm)
Change needle size if necessary to obtain correct gauge.

NOTIONS

Waste yarn

GAUGE

28 sts and 28 rows = 4″ (10 cm) in Stockinette stitch (St st)

OSTRICH PLUMES PATTERN

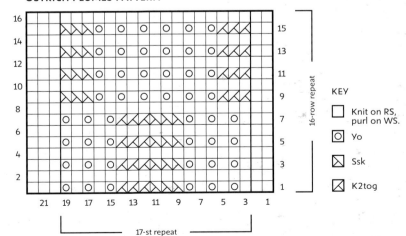

KEY

- ☐ Knit on RS, purl on WS.
- ⊙ Yo
- ⧄ Ssk
- ⧅ K2tog

17-st repeat

16-row repeat

WINTER AND SUMMER SLIPPERS

These seasonal slippers remind me of the ones I wore as a child, though the fibers used here are far more luxurious than the synthetic ones of my youth. The winter version (at left) is made with wool in a large size that is then felted down to fit; the summer version (shown on pages 82 and 83) is knitted in a breathable cotton yarn. Off the feet, their appearance is amusingly hobbit-like—especially the winter slippers, which hold their shape perfectly.

SOLE

Note: Winter slippers are worked with 2 strands of yarn held together.

Using waste yarn and provisional CO of your choice, CO 7 sts. Begin Garter st (knit every row); work even for 1 row.

Shape Sole (RS): Place marker (pm) for RS. Increase 2 sts this row, then every other row 3 times, as follows: K2, M1, knit to last 2 sts, M1, k2—15 sts. Work even until 30 (33, 36) Garter st ridges are complete on RS, ending with a WS row.

Decrease Row (RS): Decrease 2 sts this row, then every other row 3 times, as follows: K1, ssk, knit to last 3 sts, k2tog, k1—7 sts remain. Knit 1 row.

UPPER

Next Row (RS): K7, pick up and knit 34 (37, 40) sts along side edge of Sole (1 st in every Garter st ridge), carefully unpick provisional CO and k7 across these sts, pick up and knit 34 (37, 40) sts along opposite side of Sole—82 (88, 94) sts. Join for working in the rnd; pm for beginning of rnd. Begin Garter st (purl 1 rnd, knit 1 rnd); work even for 16 rnds. Change to St st (knit every rnd); work even for 1 rnd.

Next Rnd: K23 (26, 29), pm, k36, pm, knit to end.

Shape Instep: Knit to marker, slip marker (sm), k3, [sk2p, k6] 3 times, sk2p, k3, sm, knit to end—74 (80, 86) sts remain. Knit 3 rnds.

SIZES

To fit women's shoe sizes 5–6 (7–8, 9–10)

FINISHED MEASUREMENTS

Winter Slippers: 7 1/4 (8, 8 3/4)" foot length, after felting
Summer Slippers: 6 1/2 (7, 7 1/2)" foot length

YARN

Winter Slippers: St-Denis Nordique (100% wool; 150 yards / 50 grams): 2 balls #5807 Silver
Summer Slippers: Classic Elite Yarns Summer Set (64% cotton / 19% alpaca / 12% polyester / 5% lyocel; 95 yards / 50 grams): 2 balls #2178 Driftwood

NEEDLES

Winter Slippers: One set of five double-pointed needles (dpn) size US 8 (5 mm)
Summer Slippers: One set of five double-pointed needles size US 5 (3.75 mm)
Change needle size if necessary to obtain correct gauge.

NOTIONS

Waste yarn; stitch markers

GAUGE

See page 82.

GAUGE

Winter Slippers

▸ 16 sts and 28 rows = 4" (10 cm) in Garter stitch, using larger needles and 2 strands of yarn held together, before felting

▸ 18 sts and 37 rows = 4" (10 cm) in Garter stitch, using larger needles and 2 strands of yarn held together, after felting

Summer Slippers

22 sts and 42 rows = 4" (10 cm) in Garter stitch using smaller needles

Begin Short Row Shaping
(see Special Techniques, page 122)

Rows 1 and 2: Knit to marker, sm, k2, [sk2p, k4] 3 times, sk2p, k2, sm, k12, wrp-t, purl to second marker, sm, p12, wrp-t—66 (72, 78) sts remain.

Rows 3 and 4: Knit to second marker, sm, k10, wrp-t, purl to second marker, sm, p10, wrp-t.

Rows 5 and 6: Knit to marker, sm, k1, [sk2p, k2] 3 times, sk2p, k1, sm, k8, wrp-t, purl to second marker, sm, p8, wrp-t—58 (64, 70) sts remain.

Rows 7 and 8: Knit to second marker, sm, k6, wrp-t, purl to second marker, sm, p6, wrp-t.

Rows 9 and 10: Knit to marker, sm, [sk2p] 4 times, sm, k4, wrp-t, purl to second marker, sm, p4, wrp-t—50 (56, 62) sts remain.

Knit 2 rnds, working all wraps together with wrapped sts (see Special Techniques, page 122). Purl 1 rnd. Knit 1 rnd. Purl 1 rnd. BO all sts knitwise.

FINISHING

Winter Slippers

Wash slippers in washing machine at the hottest setting; for additional agitation, wash slippers with detergent and a towel. Check frequently as the felting progresses, stretching the Slipper to fit foot. Spin out excess water and reshape as necessary. Allow to dry.

Summer Slippers

Block as desired.

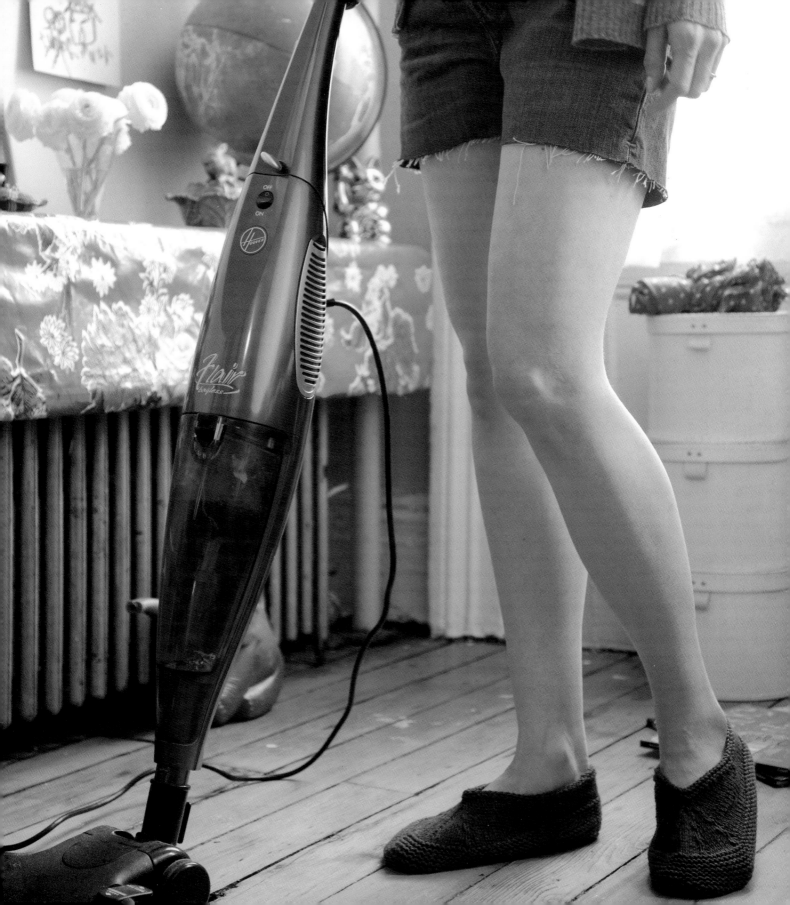

SNEAK IN A FEW ROWS

—while everyone else sleeps in

—with friends at yarn shop

—while watching soccer game

—while waiting for laundry

—as a reward for tidying up

—while keeping an eye on roast

—lounging by pool

—while catching up on phone

—watching Shakespeare in the Park

—while riding shotgun in car

weekend

FLEUR DE LYS HAT

While I originally planned to knit a straightforward ski hat, I inadvertently cast on too many stitches. Before ripping it out, I took another look and decided I liked its oversized brim. I cast on anew, this time with fewer stitches, increased toward a turning round so that the brim would flare, then decreased again to form the body of the hat. Knitting the crown is like saving the best for last—watching the design take shape is not unlike cutting snowflakes out of paper.

FINISHED MEASUREMENTS

21 ½ " circumference

YARN

JaggerSpun Heather 3/8 Sport Weight Yarn (100% medium-grade wool; 1490 yards / 1 lb): 2 ounces each Charcoal (MC) and Smoke (A)

NEEDLES

▶ One set of five double-pointed needles (dpn) size US 2 (2.75 mm)
▶ One set of five double-pointed needles size US 2 ½ (3 mm) Change needle size if necessary to obtain correct gauge.

NOTIONS

Stitch markers (one in contrasting color for beginning of rnd)

GAUGE

28 sts and 41 rnds = 4 " (10 cm) in Fair Isle Pattern from Chart, using larger needles

BRIM

Using smaller needles and A, CO 150 sts. Join for working in the rnd, being careful not to twist sts; place marker (pm) for beginning of rnd. Knit 8 rnds.

Next Rnd: *K10, M1; repeat from * to end—165 sts. Knit 4 rnds. Purl 1 rnd (turning rnd).

Change to larger needles and MC. Knit 4 rnds.

Next Rnd: *K9, k2tog; repeat from * to end—150 sts remain. Knit 9 rnds.

Next Rnd: [K30, pm] 4 times, knit to end.

Begin Pattern: Work Rnds 1–3 of Fair Isle Pattern from Chart once, Rnds 4–9 six times, then Rnds 10 and 11 once (piece should measure approximately 5 ½" from turning rnd).

Shape Crown: Work Rnds 12–36 once, working decreases as indicated in Chart—20 sts remain. *Note: Move beginning of rnd marker 1 st to the left after each decrease rnd; remove all markers after Rnd 36.*

Next Rnd: Slip 1 wyib, k1, [s2kp2, k1] 4 times, s2kp2—10 sts remain. Cut yarn, leaving a 6" long tail. Thread tail through remaining sts, pull tight and fasten off.

FINISHING

Fold Brim to WS at turning rnd and sew to WS, being careful not to let sts show on RS.

Block as desired.

FAIR ISLE CHART

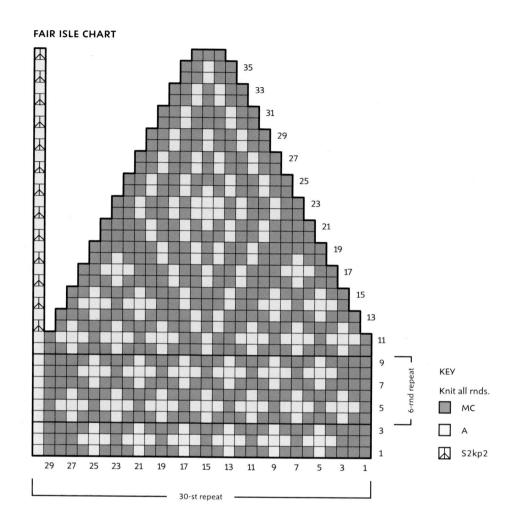

KEY

Knit all rnds.

- ▨ MC
- ☐ A
- ◩ S2kp2

ACORN TEA COZY

A knitted wool tea cozy is one of the most practical accessories for the home since it performs the very important job of keeping a teapot warm. Teapots come in a variety of sizes, so I designed this cozy with a simple 2-stitch repeating pattern that is easy to customize—simply add or remove pairs of stitches on the front and back to fit the circumference of your teapot.

STITCH PATTERN

Moss Stitch

(multiple of 2 sts + 1; 4-row repeat)

Rnd 1: K1, *p1, k1; repeat from * to end.

Rnds 2 and 3: P1, *k1, p1; repeat from * to end.

Rnd 4: Repeat Rnd 1.

Repeat Rnds 1–4 for Moss Stitch.

TEA COZY

Using circ needle, CO 46 sts, place marker (pm) for side, CO 46 sts—92 sts. Join for working in the rnd, being careful not to twist sts; pm for beginning of rnd.

Rnd 1: [Slip 1, purl to marker] twice.

Rnd 2: Knit.

Repeat Rnds 1 and 2 seven times.

Rnd 3: [Slip 1, work in Moss st to marker] twice.

Rnd 4: [K1, work to marker] twice.

Repeat Rnds 3 and 4 until piece measures 5½".

Shape Top: *Note: Change to dpns when necessary for number of sts on needle.* Decrease 4 sts this rnd, every other rnd 11 times, then every rnd 9 times, as follows: *Work 1 st, work 2 sts together (k2tog if next st should be a knit st, or p2tog if next st should be a purl st), work to 3 sts before marker, work 2 sts together (ssk if next st should be a knit st, or ssp if next st should be a purl st); repeat from * once—8 sts remain.

Next Rnd: [K2tog] 4 times—4 sts remain. Remove markers.

FINISHING

Transfer remaining sts to single dpn. Work I-Cord (see Special Techniques, page 122) for 3". Cut yarn, leaving an 8" tail. Thread tail through remaining sts, pull tight and fasten off. Using tail, sew end of I-Cord to its base to form a loop.

Block as desired.

FINISHED MEASUREMENTS

▶ 23" circumference
▶ 10" high, not including loop

YARN

Classic Elite Duchess (40% merino wool / 28% viscose / 15% nylon / 10% cashmere / 7% angora; 75 yards / 50 grams): 3 balls #1076 Baronet's Brown

NEEDLES

▶ One 24" (60 cm) long circular (circ) needle size US 8 (5 mm)
▶ One set of five double-pointed needles (dpn) size US 8 (5 mm)
Change needle size if necessary to obtain correct gauge.

NOTIONS

Stitch markers (one in contrasting color for beginning of rnd)

GAUGE

16 sts and 28 rnds = 4" (10 cm) in Moss Stitch

TOE-UP TRADITIONAL SOCKS

My father-in-law used to love the socks I would knit for him, but I always feared that I would run out of yarn before completing the toes when knitting for his size 11 feet. Then I discovered toe-up socks; simply divide your yarn in half (one half for each sock), start at the toes, and keep knitting until the yarn runs out. This is helpful when making socks for people with large feet, but it also helps those with daintier extremities when yarn is limited. Most toe-up patterns use short rows for the heels, which only offers a single layer of fabric. To make these socks more durable, I reinforced the heel with slipped stitches, which are typically only used in traditional top-down socks.

STITCH PATTERN

2x2 Rib

(multiple of 4 sts; 1-rnd repeat)
All Rnds: *K2, p2; repeat from * to end.

TOE

Using waste yarn and provisional CO of your choice, CO 16 sts. Divide sts evenly among 4 needles. Join for working in the rnd, being careful not to twist sts; place marker (pm) for beginning of rnd. Begin St st (knit every rnd); work even for 1 rnd.

Shape Toe

Increase Rnd: *Needle 1:* K1, M1, knit to end; *Needle 2:* Knit to last st, M1, k1; *Needles 3 and 4:* Repeat Needles 1 and 2—20 sts.

Repeat Increase Rnd every rnd 6 times, then every other rnd 7 times—72 sts.

FOOT

Work even until piece measures 3 ½" less than desired length from Toe.

Gusset

Increase Rnd: *Needles 1 and 2:* Work even as established; *Needle 3:* M1, knit to end; *Needle 4:* Knit to last st, M1, k1—74 sts. Work even for 1 rnd.

Repeat Increase Rnd every other rnd 10 times, then every rnd once—96 sts (18-18-30-30).

Turn Heel

Next Row (RS): *Needles 1 and 2:* Knit; *Needle 3:* K18; *Spare Needle:* K12 from Needle 3, k12 from Needle 4, leaving remaining 18 sts on Needle 4 for Heel Flap.

Row 1 (WS): Working only on 24 sts on Spare Needle, purl to end.

SIZES

To fit women's shoe sizes 6–10

FINISHED MEASUREMENTS

▸ 7 ¾" Foot circumference
▸ 9 ½" Foot length from back of Heel
▸ 9" Leg length to base of Heel

YARN

Schaefer Anne (60% superwash merino wool / 25% mohair / 15% nylon; 560 yards / 4 ounces): 1 hank Red/Cinnamon/Ochre

NEEDLES

One set of six double-pointed needles (dpn) size US 0 (2 mm) Change needle size if necessary to obtain correct gauge.

NOTIONS

Waste yarn, stitch marker

GAUGE

37 sts and 46 rnds = 4" (10 cm) in Stockinette stitch (St st)

Row 2: K1, k2tog, knit to last 3 sts, ssk, k1.

Repeat Rows 1 and 2 eight times—6 sts remain. Cut yarn.

HEEL FLAP

Set-Up Row (RS): With RS facing, using empty needle (Needle 5), rejoin yarn to right side of Heel, pick up and knit 15 sts along right side of Heel, knit across 6 Heel sts, pick up and knit 15 sts along left side of Heel—36 sts on Needle 5. Slip first st on Needle 4 onto Needle 5, pass next-to-last st on Needle 5 over last st, turn.

Row 1: Slip 1, purl to last st, p2tog (last st on Needle 5 together with first st on Needle 3), turn.

Row 2: *Slip 1, k1; repeat from * to last 2 sts, slip 1, ssk (last st on Needle 5 together with first st on Needle 4).

Repeat Rows 1 and 2 sixteen times, then Row 1 once—36 sts on Needle 5, 0 sts remain on Needles 3 and 4. Redistribute sts evenly among 4 needles—72 sts. Rejoin for working in the rnd, pm for beginning of rnd.

LEG

Continuing in St st, work even until Leg measures 5″ from end of Heel Flap. Change to 2x2 Rib; work even for 1 ½″. BO all sts in pattern.

FINISHING

Carefully unpick waste yarn from provisional CO and divide sts evenly onto 2 needles (8 sts for top of Toe, 8 sts for bottom). Using Kitchener st (see Special Techniques, page 122), graft Toe sts.

Block as desired.

MESH LAYERING TANK

This lacy tank is summer's answer to the sweater vest. It is an ideal layering piece and an easy way to dress up an otherwise casual outfit. Wear it over a silk camisole or a contrasting long-sleeved tee, depending on the weather. The hemp yarn and open stitch pattern breathe easily, keeping you cool in warm weather while adding a pop of color and texture.

STITCH PATTERN

English Mesh Lace

(multiple of 6 sts; 8-rnd repeat)

Rnd 1: *Yo, ssk, k1, k2tog, yo, k1; repeat from * to end.

Rnd 2 and All Even-Numbered Rnds: Knit.

Rnd 3: *Yo, k1, sk2p, k1, yo, k1; repeat from * to end.

Rnd 5: *K2tog, yo, k1, yo, ssk, k1; repeat from * to end, remove marker, k1 from next rnd, replace marker for new beginning of rnd.

Rnd 7: *[K1, yo] twice, k1, sk2p; repeat from * to end.

Rnd 8: Knit.

Repeat Rnds 1–8 for English Mesh Lace.

BODY

Using larger needle, CO 204 (228, 252, 276, 300, 324) sts. Join for working in the rnd, being careful not to twist sts; place marker (pm) for beginning of rnd. Begin English Mesh Lace; work even until piece measures 15 (15, 15, 16, 16, 16)" from the beginning, ending with Rnd 7 of English Mesh Lace.

Divide for Front and Back (WS): P6 (6, 6, 12, 12, 18) and place on holder for left underarm, p89 (101, 113, 113, 125, 125) sts for Back. Place next 13 (13, 13, 25, 25, 37) sts on holder for right underarm, following 89 (101, 113, 113, 125, 125) sts on separate holder for Front, then remaining 7 (7, 7, 13, 13, 19) sts on same holder as left underarm sts.

BACK

Shape Armholes (RS): Work Rows 1–8 of Decrease Chart, working decreases as indicated—77 (89, 101, 101, 113, 113) sts remain.

Shape Armholes and Neck (RS): Work Row 1 of Decrease Chart across next 29 (29, 29, 29, 41, 41) sts; join a second ball of yarn, k19 (31, 43, 43, 31, 31) and place on holder for neck, work Row 1 of Decrease Chart to end—27 (27, 27, 27, 39, 39) sts remain each side. Working left side of neck only, continue working decreases as indicated in Chart, working Rows 2–8 once, Rows 1–8 zero (0, 0, 0, 1, 1) time(s), then Rows 9–18 once—3

SIZES

X-Small (Small, Medium, Large, 1X-Large, 2X-Large)

FINISHED MEASUREMENTS

32 ¾ (36 ½, 40 ¼, 44 ¼, 48, 51 ¾)" bust

YARN

Lanaknits Designs allhemp3 (100% hemp; 165 yards / 50 grams): 4 (4, 4, 5, 5, 6) hanks #022 Pumpkin

NEEDLES

▸ One 32" (80 cm) long or longer circular (circ) needle size US 2 (2.75 mm)

▸ One 32" (80 cm) long circular needle size US 1 (2.25 mm)

▸ One 16" (40 cm) or 20" (50 cm) long circular needle size US 1 (2.25 mm)

Change needle size if necessary to obtain correct gauge.

NOTIONS

Stitch markers; stitch holders

GAUGE

25 sts and 34 rnds = 4" (10 cm) in English Mesh Lace, using larger needle

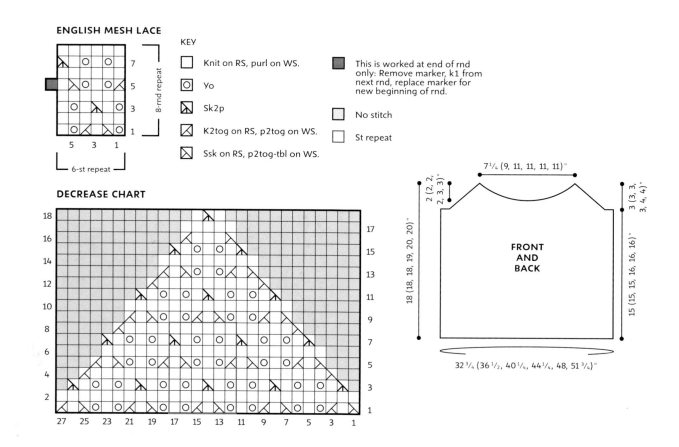

ENGLISH MESH LACE

KEY

□	Knit on RS, purl on WS.
⊚	Yo
⧅	Sk2p
⊠	K2tog on RS, p2tog on WS.
⊠	Ssk on RS, p2tog-tbl on WS.

■ This is worked at end of rnd only: Remove marker, k1 from next rnd, replace marker for new beginning of rnd.

□ No stitch

□ St repeat

DECREASE CHART

sts remain. Cut yarn, leaving 6″ tail. Thread tail through remaining sts, pull tight and fasten off. Repeat for right side.

FRONT

With WS facing, rejoin yarn to sts on hold for Front. Purl 1 row. Complete as for Back.

FINISHING

Neckband and Strap: With RS facing, using smaller 32″ long circ needle, pick up and knit 13 sts from right Back neck edge, knit across 19 (31, 43, 43, 55, 55) sts on hold for Back neck, pick up and knit 13 sts from left Back neck edge, CO 60 sts for Left Strap, pick up and knit 13 sts from left Front neck edge, knit across 19 (31, 43, 43, 55, 55) sts on hold for Front neck, pick up and knit 13 sts from right Front neck edge, CO 60 sts for Right Strap—210 (234, 258, 258, 282, 282) sts. Join for working in the rnd, being careful not to twist CO sts; pm for beginning of rnd. Begin Garter st (purl 1 rnd, knit 1 rnd); work even for 5 rnds. BO all sts purlwise.

Armhole Edging and Strap: With RS facing, beginning on left side of Front, using smaller 16″ or 20″ circ needle, pick up and knit 18 sts along left Front armhole edge, knit across 13 (13, 13, 25, 25, 37) sts from holder for left underarm, pick up and knit 18 sts along left Back armhole edge, then pick up and knit 59 sts from CO edge of Strap—108 (108, 108, 120, 120, 132) sts. Begin Garter st; work even for 5 rnds. BO all sts purlwise.

Block as desired.

REDWORK COWL AND MITTS

Red and cream stripes merrily decorate this cowl-and-mitts duo, while little buttons add equal parts style and function. This particular angora and alpaca yarn is available in more than three dozen colors, providing ample opportunities to make cowl-and-mitt duos to complement the palette of any outfit in your closet.

ABBREVIATIONS

RC (right cross): Slip 2 sts to cn, hold to back, k1, k2 from cn.

LC (left cross): Slip next st to cn, hold to front, k2, k1 from cn.

STITCH PATTERN

Gull Wing Pattern

(multiple of 6 sts; 2-rnd repeat)

Rnd 1: K2, slip 2 wyib, k2.

Rnd 2: Slip 2 sts to cn, hold to back, k1, [k1, slip 1 wyib from cn], slip next st to cn, hold to front, slip 1 wyib, k1, k1 from cn.

Repeat Rnds 1 and 2 for Gull Wing Pattern.

RIGHT MITT

CUFF

Using dpns and MC, CO 56 (60, 64) sts. Do not join. Begin Garter st (knit every row); work even for 2 rows.

Buttonhole Row (RS): Continuing in Garter st, make buttonhole this row, then every 6 rows 3 times, as follows: K2, yo, k2tog, knit to end. Work even for 3 rows.

HAND

Divide sts among 4 dpns [12-12-24-8 (13-13-26-8, 14-14-28-8)].

Rnd 1: Join for working in the rnd as follows: Hold Needle 4 parallel to and behind Needle 1, [k2tog] 8 times (1 st from Needle 1 together with 1 st from Needle 4), knit to end—48 (52, 56) sts remain. Transfer last 12 (13, 14) sts from Needle 3 to Needle 4. Place marker (pm) for beginning of rnd. Change to A; knit 1 rnd.

Next Rnd: K1 (2, 3), [pm, work Gull Wing Pattern across next 6 sts, pm, k2] twice, pm, work Gull Wing Pattern across next 6 sts, pm, k1 (2, 3), pm for side, knit to end. Work even for 7 rnds, changing colors every Rnd 2 of pattern.

Shape Hand

Note: Hand shaping and Thumb Opening are worked at the same time. Please read entire section through before beginning.

FINISHED MEASUREMENTS

Mitts: Approximately 6 ½ (7, 7 ½)" hand circumference

Cowl: 16 ½" circumference, buttoned

YARN

Classic Elite Yarns Fresco (60% wool / 30% baby alpaca / 10% angora; 164 yards / 50 grams): 1 hank each #5355 Rumba Red (MC) and #5336 Oatmeal (A) *(Note: 1 hank each color will make both Mitts and Cowl.)*

NEEDLES

Mitts: One set of five double-pointed needles (dpn) size US 1 (2.25 mm)

Cowl: One 16" (40 cm) long circular (circ) needle size US 3 (3.25 mm)

Change needle size if necessary to obtain correct gauge.

NOTIONS

Mitts: Stitch markers (one in contrasting color for beginning of rnd); waste yarn; cable needle (cn); eight ³/₈" buttons

Cowl: Six ½" buttons

GAUGE

Mitts: 14 ½ sts and 22 rows = 2" (5 cm) in Stockinette stitch (St st), using smaller needles

Cowl: 24 sts and 37 rows = 4" (10 cm) in Stockinette stitch, using larger needles

Increase Rnd 1: K1, M1, work to 1 st before side marker, M1, k1, sm, k1, M1, knit to last st, M1, k1—52 (56, 60) sts. Work even for 3 rnds.

Increase Rnd 2: Work to second marker, sm, M1, work to fifth marker, M1, sm, work to side marker, sm, k1, M1, knit to last st, M1, k1—56 (60, 64) sts. Work even for 3 rnds.

Increase Rnd 3: K1, M1, work to 1 st before side marker, M1, k1, sm, k1, M1, knit to last st, M1, k1—60 (64, 68) sts. Work even for 3 rnds.

Repeat last 8 rnds once, then repeat Increase Rnd 3 once—72 (76, 80) sts.

Thumb Opening
AT THE SAME TIME, when piece measures 3 ½" from beginning of Hand, work to side marker, transfer next 8 sts to waste yarn for Thumb, CO 8 sts, work to end. Work even until piece measures 3 ¾ (4, 4 ¼)" from beginning of Hand, ending with Rnd 1 of Gull Wing Pattern in A. Cut A.

Decrease Rnd: K1 (2, 3), [ssk] twice, sm, RC, LC, sm, k2tog, k2, sm, RC, LC, sm, k2, ssk, RC, LC, sm, [k2tog] twice, k1 (2, 3), sm, k1 (2, 3), [ssk] 3 times, knit to last 7 (8, 9) sts, [k2tog] 3 times, k1 (2, 3)—60 (64, 68) sts remain. Change to Garter st (purl 1 rnd, knit 1 rnd); work even for 8 rnds. BO all sts purlwise.

THUMB
Transfer sts from waste yarn to dpn. Pick up (but do not knit) 2 sts before CO sts, 4 sts from CO sts, pm for beginning of rnd, 4 sts from CO sts, then 1 st after CO sts—19 sts. Rejoin yarn at marker. Join for working in the rnd. Begin Garter st; work even for 6 rnds. BO all sts purlwise.

LEFT MITT
CUFF
Using dpns and MC, CO 56 (60, 64) sts. Do not join. Begin Garter st; work even for 2 rows.

Buttonhole Row (RS): Continuing in Garter st, make buttonhole this row, then every 6 rows 3 times as follows: Knit to last 4 sts, k2tog, yo, k2. Work even for 3 rows. Cut yarn.

HAND

Distribute sts among 4 dpns [8-24-12-12 (8-26-13-13, 8-28-14-14)].

Rnd 1: Join for working in the rnd as follows: Hold Needle 1 parallel to and behind Needle 4, rejoin yarn and knit across Needles 2 and 3, k4, [k2tog] 8 times (1 st from Needle 4 together with 1 st from Needle 1), knit to end—48 (52, 56) sts remain. Transfer first 12 (13, 14) sts from Needle 2 onto Needle 1. Place marker for beginning of rnd. Change to A; knit 1 rnd.

Next Rnd: K24 (26, 28), pm for side, k1 (2, 3), [pm, work Gull Wing Pattern across next 6 sts, pm, k2] twice, pm, work Gull Wing Pattern across next 6 sts, pm, k1 (2, 3). Work even for 7 rnds, changing colors every Rnd 2 of pattern.

Shape Hand

Note: Hand shaping and Thumb Opening are worked at the same time. Please read entire section through before beginning.

Increase Rnd 1: K1, M1, knit to 1 st before side marker, M1, k1, sm, k1, M1, knit to last st, sm, M1, k1—52 (56, 60) sts. Work even for 3 rnds.

Increase Rnd 2: K1, M1, knit to 1 st before side marker, M1, k1, sm, work to third marker, sm, M1, work to fifth marker, sm, M1, work to end—56 (60, 64) sts. Work even for 3 rnds.

Increase Rnd 3: K1, M1, knit to 1 st before side marker, M1, k1, sm, k1, M1, knit to last st, M1, k1—60 (64, 68) sts. Work even for 3 rnds.

Repeat last 8 rnds once, then repeat Increase Rnd 3 once—72 (76, 80) sts.

Thumb Opening

AT THE SAME TIME, when piece measures 3 ½″ from beginning of Hand, work to 8 sts before side marker, transfer next 8 sts to waste yarn for Thumb, CO 8 sts, work to end. Work even until piece measures 3 ¾ (4, 4 ¼)″ from beginning of Hand, ending with Rnd 1 of Gull Wing Pattern in A. Cut A.

Decrease Rnd: K1 (2, 3), [ssk] three times, knit to 7 (8, 9) sts before side seam marker, [k2tog] three times, k1 (2, 3), sm, k1 (2, 3), [ssk] twice, sm, RC, LC, sm, k2tog, k2, sm, RC, LC, sm, k2, ssk, RC, LC, sm, [k2tog] twice, k1 (2, 3)—60 (64, 68) sts remain. Change to Garter st; work even for 8 rnds. BO all sts purlwise.

THUMB

Complete as for Right Mitt.

FINISHING

Sew buttons opposite buttonholes.

Block as desired.

COWL

Using circ needle and MC, CO 118 sts. Begin Garter st (knit every row); work even for 3 rows.

Buttonhole Row: Make buttonhole this row, then every 10 rows 5 times, as follows: K3, yo, k2tog, knit to end. Work even for 6 rows.

Next Row (RS): K6 in MC, k106 in A, join a second ball of MC, k6 in MC. Keeping first and last 6 sts in MC and Garter st, work in St st across center 106 sts, changing colors over center sts every RS row; work even for 37 rows. Change to MC and Garter st; work even for 9 rows. BO all sts knitwise.

FINISHING

Sew buttons opposite buttonholes.

Block as desired.

HEILO MITTENS

Not surprisingly, mittens are a favorite project for many knitters—they're both practical for cold weather and the perfect canvas to showcase a fancy or colorful technique. This simple pair uses two neutral shades of wool with a bit of red at the cuff to spice things up. The motif can be memorized easily so you'll hardly need to check the chart once you get going.

FINISHED MEASUREMENTS
Approximately 8 ¼ " hand circumference

YARN
Dale of Norway Heilo (100% wool; 109 yards / 50 grams): 2 skeins #0020 Natural (A); 1 skein each #3841 Medium Sheep's Heather (B) and #4146 Wine (C)

NEEDLES
One set of five double-pointed needles (dpn) size US 2 ½ (3 mm) Change needle size if necessary to obtain correct gauge.

NOTIONS
Stitch marker; waste yarn

GAUGE
32 sts and 31 rnds = 4 " (10 cm) in Fair Isle pattern from Back of Hand Chart

RIGHT MITTEN

CUFF

With B, CO 56 sts. Join for working in the rnd, being careful not to twist sts; place marker (pm) for beginning of rnd.

Begin Latvian Braid
Rnd 1: *K1 with B, k1 with C; repeat from * to end.

Rnd 2: Holding both strands in front of work, and bringing the working strand over the non-working strand for each st, *p1 with B, p1 with C; repeat from * to end.

Rnd 3: Holding both strands in front of work, and bringing the working strand under the non-working strand for each st, *p1 with B, p1 with C; repeat from * to end.

Begin Pattern: Begin Cuff Chart; work Rnds 1–16 of Chart once.

HAND

Shape Hand and Thumb: Work across Back of Hand Chart, then across Palm Chart; work Rnds 1–13 once, working increases as indicated in Charts—66 sts.

Thumb Opening
Next Rnd: Working Rnd 14 of Charts, work 35 sts in pattern, change to waste yarn and k11, slip these 11 sts back to left-hand needle, change to working yarn and work remaining sts from Charts.

Mitten Top
Work even until both Charts have been completed, working decreases as indicated in Charts—10 sts remain. Divide sts evenly onto 2 needles. Using Kitchener st (see Special Techniques, page 122), graft sts.

THUMB

Carefully remove waste yarn from Thumb sts and place bottom 11 sts and top 10 sts onto 2 dpns, being careful not to twist sts. Join A and B to bottom sts and, working Thumb Chart, pick up and knit 2 sts at side of Thumb Opening, knit across bottom sts, pick up and knit 3 sts at other side of Thumb Opening, knit across top sts—26 sts. Redistribute sts evenly among 3 dpns. Join for working in the rnd; pm for beginning of rnd. Continue Thumb Chart; work even until entire Chart has been completed, working decreases as indicated in Chart—6 sts remain. Divide sts evenly onto 2 needles. Using Kitchener st, graft sts.

LEFT MITTEN

Work as for Right Mitten to beginning of Hand.

HAND

Shape Hand and Thumb: Work across Palm Chart, beginning with st 25 and working in reverse to st 1, work across Back of Hand Chart; work Rnds 1–13 once, working increases as indicated in Charts—66 sts.

Thumb Opening

Next Rnd: Working Rnd 14 of Charts, work 20 sts in pattern, change to waste yarn and k11, slip these 11 sts back to left-hand needle, change to working yarn and work remaining sts from Charts.

Complete as for Right Mitten. *Note: When picking up sts for Thumb, pick up 3 sts at first side of Thumb opening and 2 sts at opposite side.*

FINISHING

Block as desired.

CUFF CHART

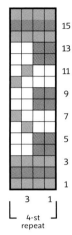

3   1
⎿ 4-st ⏌
repeat

THUMB CHART

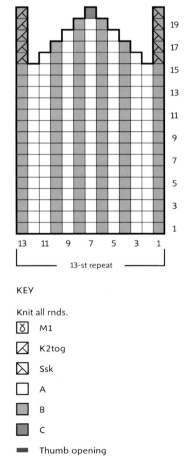

13 11 9 7 5 3 1

⎿___ 13-st repeat ___⏌

KEY

Knit all rnds.

⊠ M1

⊠ K2tog

⊠ Ssk

☐ A

▦ B

▦ C

▬ Thumb opening

BACK OF HAND CHART

PALM CHART

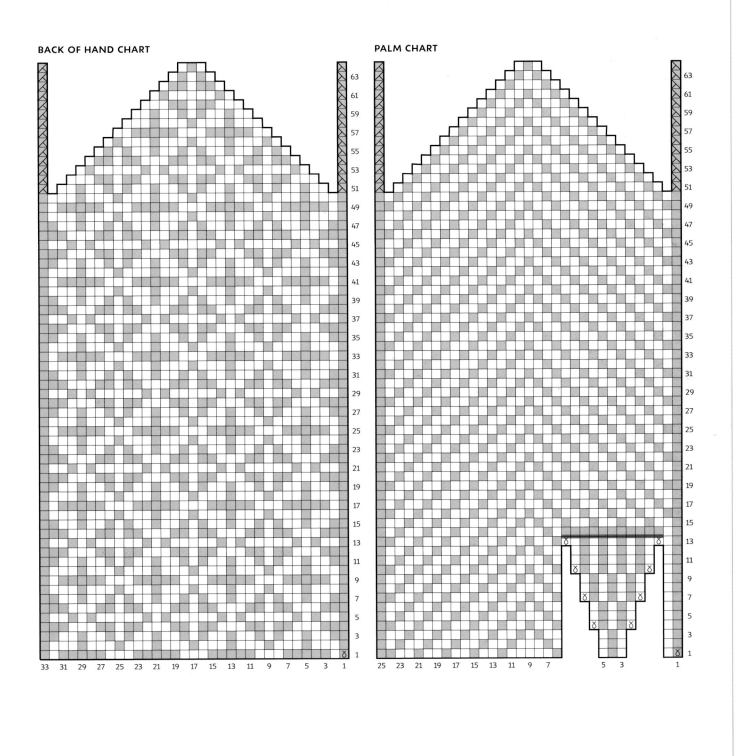

ROPES AND LADDERS HEADBAND

Fastened at the nape of the neck, this pretty headband is a simple way to dress up an outfit—especially if you put up your hair to show off the charmingly mismatched vintage buttons.

FIRST HALF

CO 22 sts. Knit 1 row. Begin pattern from Chart; work even until piece measures 4 ¾″ from the beginning, ending with a WS row.

Shape Headband

Decrease Row 1 (RS): Decrease 2 sts this row, then every other row twice, as follows: Work 7 sts, ssp, work to last 9 sts, p2tog, work to end—16 sts. Work even for 1 row.

Decrease Row 2 (RS): Work 6 sts, ssp, p2tog, work to end—14 sts remain. Work even for 1 row.

Decrease Row 3 (RS): Work 6 sts, p2tog, work to end—13 sts remain. Work even through Row 1 of Chart.

Next Row (WS): Work 3 sts, p3tog, p1, p3tog, work to end—9 sts remain. Change to Garter st (knit every row); work even until piece measures 8 ¼″, ending with a WS row.

Buttonhole Row (RS): K3, k2tog, yo, k3. Work even for 13 rows. Repeat Buttonhole Row once. Work even for 1 row.

Shape Tip

Decrease Row 1 (RS): K3, s2kp2, k3—7 sts remain. Work even for 1 row.

Decrease Row 2 (RS): K2, s2kp2, k2—5 sts remain. Work even for 1 row.

Decrease Row 3 (RS): K1, s2kp2, k1—3 sts remain. Work even for 1 row. Cut yarn, leaving an 8″ tail. Thread tail through remaining sts, pull tight, and fasten off.

SECOND HALF

With RS facing, pick up and knit 22 sts from CO row of First Half. Complete as for First Half, omitting buttonholes.

FINISHING

Sew buttons to end opposite buttonholes, adjusting fit as necessary by adjusting placement of buttons.

Block as desired.

FINISHED MEASUREMENTS

2 ¾″ wide x 18 ½″ circumference, buttoned

YARN

St-Denis Nordique (100% wool; 150 yards / 50 grams): 1 ball #5801 White

NEEDLES

One pair straight needles size US 3 (3.25 mm)
Change needle size if necessary to obtain correct gauge.

NOTIONS

Two ⅝″ buttons

GAUGE

22 sts and 23 rows = 2 ¾″ (7 cm) in pattern from Chart

CHART

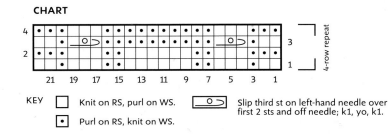

KEY
☐ Knit on RS, purl on WS.
▪ Purl on RS, knit on WS.
⬭ Slip third st on left-hand needle over first 2 sts and off needle; k1, yo, k1.

188

remarks. As these had not been well received, he had desisted. Even he was sensible of the decorous atmosphere and even he began to respond to the religious stimulus. In a whisper, Mr. Cunningham drew Mr. Kernan's attention to Mr. Harford, the moneylender, who sat some distance off, and to Mr. Fanning, the registration agent and mayor maker of the city, who was sitting immediately under the pulpit beside one of the newly elected councillors of the ward. To the right sat old Michael Grimes, the owner of three pawnbroker's shops, and Dan Hogan's nephew, who was up for the job in the Town Clerk's office. Farther in front sat Mr. Hendrick, the chief reporter of *The Freeman's Journal*, and poor O'Carroll, an old friend of Mr. Kernan's, had been at one time a considerable commercial figure. Gradually, as he recognised familiar faces, Mr. Kernan began to feel more at home. His hat, which had been rehabilitated by his wife, rested upon his knees. Once or twice he pulled down his cuffs with one hand while he held the brim of his hat lightly, but firmly, with the other hand.

A powerful-looking figure, the upper part of which was draped with a white surplice, was observed to be struggling up into the pulpit. Immediately the congregation unsettled, produced handkerchiefs and knelt upon them with care. Mr. Kernan followed the general example. The priest's figure now stood upright in the pulpit, two-thirds of its bulk, crowned by a massive red face, appearing above the balustrade.

Father Purdon knelt down, turned towards the red speck of light and, covering his face with his hands, prayed. After an interval, he uncovered his face and rose. The congregation rose also and settled again on its benches. Mr. Kernan restored his hat to its original position on his knee and presented an attentive face to

the preacher. The preacher turned back each wide sleeve of his surplice with an elaborate large gesture and slowly surveyed the array of faces. Then he said:

"For the children of this world are wiser in their generation than the children of light. Wherefore make unto yourselves friends out of the mammon of iniquity so that when you die they may receive you into everlasting dwellings."

Father Purdon developed the text with resonant assurance. It was one of the most difficult texts in all the Scriptures, he said, to interpret properly. It was a text which might seem to the casual observer at variance with the lofty morality elsewhere preached by Jesus Christ. But, he told his hearers, the text had seemed to him specially adapted for the guidance of those whose lot it was to lead the life of the world and who yet wished to lead that life not in the manner of worldlings. It was a text for business men and professional men. Jesus Christ, with His divine understanding of every cranny of our human nature, understood that all men were not called to the religious life, that by far the vast majority were forced to live in the world, and, to a certain extent, for the world: and in this sentence He designed to give them a word of counsel, setting before them as exemplars in the religious life those very worshippers of Mammon who were of all men the least solicitous in matters religious.

He told his hearers that he was there that evening for no terrifying, no extravagant purpose; but as a man of the world speaking to his fellow-men. He came to speak to business men and he would speak to them in a businesslike way. If he might use the metaphor, he said, he was their spiritual accountant, and he wished each

189

SEA CREST BOOKMARK

This quick-to-knit bookmark makes a thoughtful gift for an avid reader. Decreases and yarnovers along both sides create gentle waves, and craft felt fused to the back gives it body and prevents the edges from rolling under.

BOOKMARK
CO 1 st.

Shape Bottom Tip
Row 1 (RS): K1-f/b—2 sts.

Row 2 and all WS rows: Purl.

Row 3: Increase 1 st at end of this row, then every other row 13 times, as follows: Knit to last st, k1-f/b—16 sts. Work even for 1 row.

Begin Pattern (RS): Work Rows 1–10 of Chart 5 times, omitting all yarnovers on last repeat of Chart—6 sts remain.

Shape Top Tip
Row 1 (RS): Knit to last 2 sts, ssk—5 sts remain.

Row 2: Ssp, purl to end—4 sts remain.

Repeat last 2 rows once—2 sts remain. Cut yarn, thread tail through remaining sts, pull tight and fasten off.

FINISHING
Block as desired. Following manufacturer's instructions, use iron-on adhesive to fuse bookmark to felt. Allow to cool. Trim felt.

FINISHED MEASUREMENTS
Approximately 2" x 9"

YARN
St-Denis Nordique (100% wool; 150 yards / 50 grams): 1 balls #5820 Blue Eggshell

NEEDLES
One pair straight needles size US 2 (2.75 mm)

NOTIONS
Iron-on adhesive; 4" x 10" piece of craft felt

GAUGE
13 sts and 18 rows = 2" (5 cm) in Stockinette stitch (St st)
Note: Gauge is not essential for this project.

CHART

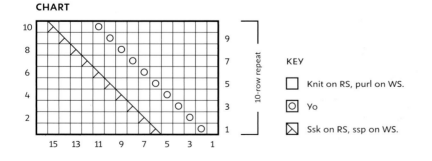

10-row repeat

KEY

☐ Knit on RS, purl on WS.

◻ Yo

⧄ Ssk on RS, ssp on WS.

LACY CABLE SOCKS

As handsome as heavily cabled socks are, most shoes just won't accommodate them. Instead, I prefer to work this easy lace pattern that has the look of cables without the bulk. The heel flap is worked in Garter stitch with all stitches knitted through the back loop. This prevents the Garter stitch from expanding and is a great way to reinforce the heel.

NOTES

When picking up sts along the side of the Heel Flap, pick up the leading "leg" of each slipped st with the left-hand needle and knit the st through the back loop.

LEG

CO 64 sts. Knit 1 row. Divide sts evenly among 4 needles. Join for working in the rnd, being careful not to twist sts; place marker (pm) for beginning of rnd. Begin Garter st (purl 1 rnd, knit 1 rnd); work even for 6 rnds.

Next Rnd: Change to Lace Pattern from Chart; work Rnds 1–8 of Chart 10 times (piece should measure approximately 7 ¾" from the beginning).

HEEL FLAP

Slip sts from Needle 2 to Needle 1, removing marker. Leave remaining 32 sts on 2 needles for instep. Work back and forth on Needles 1 and 2 only.

Row 1 (RS): Slip 1, *k1-tbl; repeat from * to end.

SIZES

To fit women's shoe sizes 6–10

FINISHED MEASUREMENTS

▸ 8 " Foot circumference
▸ 9 ½ " Foot length from back of Heel
▸ 9 ¾ " Leg length to base of Heel

YARN

Kid Hollow Farm Sock Yarn (48% kid mohair / 30% merino / 22% nylon; 104 yards / 1 ounce): 3 ¾ ounces Golden Pear

NEEDLES

One set of five double-pointed needles (dpn) size US 0 (2 mm) Change needle size if necessary to obtain correct gauge.

NOTIONS

Stitch marker

GAUGE

30 sts and 42 rnds = 4 " (10 cm) in Stockinette stitch (St st)

LACE PATTERN

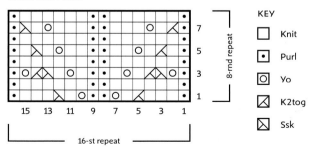

KEY

☐ Knit
▪ Purl
⊙ Yo
⧄ K2tog
⧅ Ssk

Row 2: Slip 1 wyif, *k1-tbl; repeat from * to last st, p1.

Repeat Rows 1 and 2 fourteen times.

Turn Heel

Set-Up Row 1 (RS): Slip 1, k17, ssk, k1, turn.

Set-Up Row 2: Slip 1, p5, p2tog, p1, turn.

Row 1: Slip 1, knit to 1 st before gap, ssk (the 2 sts on either side of gap), k1, turn.

Row 2: Slip 1, purl to 1 st before gap, p2tog (the 2 sts on either side of gap), p1, turn.

Repeat Rows 1 and 2 five times, omitting the final k1 and p1 sts in the last repeat of Rows 1 and 2—18 sts remain.

Gusset

Next Row (RS): *Needle 1:* Slip 1, knit across Heel Flap sts, pick up and knit 15 sts along left side of Heel Flap, pick up and knit 1 st from row below first st on Needle 2; *Needles 2 and 3:* Continue Lace Pattern from Chart as established; *Needle 4:* Pick up and knit 1 st from row below first Heel Flap st, pick up and knit 15 sts along left side of Heel Flap, k9 from Needle 1. Join for working in the rnd; pm for beginning of rnd—82 sts (25-16-16-25).

Decrease Rnd: *Needle 1:* Knit to last 3 sts, k2tog, k1; *Needles 2 and 3:* Work even as established; *Needle 4:* K1, ssk, knit to end—80 sts remain. Work even for 1 rnd.

Repeat Decrease Rnd every other rnd 8 times—64 sts remain (16-16-16-16).

FOOT

Work even until Foot measures 2″ less than desired length from back of Heel, ending with an even-numbered rnd of Chart. Change to Garter st, beginning with a purl rnd; work even for 5 rnds.

TOE

Decrease Rnd: *Needle 1:* Knit to last 3 sts, ssk, k1; *Needle 2:* K1, k2tog, knit to end; *Needle 3:* Knit to last 3 sts, skp, k1; *Needle 4:* K1, k2tog, knit to end—60 sts remain. Purl 1 rnd.

Repeat last 2 rnds 11 times—16 sts remain. Knit to end of Needle 1.

FINISHING

Break yarn, leaving long tail. Transfer sts from Needle 1 to Needle 4, and sts from Needle 3 to Needle 2. Using Kitchener st (see Special Techniques, page 122), graft Toe sts.

Block as desired.

CABLED GLOVES

These gloves are cousins to the Cabled Beret on page 41 in that they use the same yarn and similar cables. Quickly worked up using only two balls of yarn, they make an ideal present. For an especially nice gift, make the beret in a matching color to complete the set.

NOTES

Size Small/Medium Gloves are worked on size US 2 needles; size Large are worked on size US 3 needles. Instructions are given for both sizes. Instructions for size Small/Medium are given first, instructions for size Large are given in parentheses; where there is only one set of figures, it applies to both sizes.

ABBREVIATIONS

LT (left twist): Slip next st to cn, hold to front, k1, k1 from cn.
RT (right twist): Slip next st to cn, hold to back, k1, k1 from cn.

STITCH PATTERNS

Left Cable

(multiple of 4 sts; 4-rnd repeat)
Rnd 1: *P1, slip 1 wyib, k1, p1; repeat from * to end.
Rnd 2: *P1, LT, p1; repeat from * to end.
Rnds 3 and 4: *P1, k2, p1; repeat from * to end.
Repeat Rnds 1–4 for Left Cable.

Right Cable

(multiple of 4 sts; 4-rnd repeat)
Rnd 1: *P1, k1, slip 1 wyib, p1; repeat from * to end.
Rnd 2: *P1, RT, p1; repeat from * to end.
Rnds 3 and 4: *P1, k2, p1; repeat from * to end.
Repeat Rnds 1–4 for Right Cable.

LEFT GLOVE

Cuff

Using smaller (larger) needles, CO 48 sts, divide sts evenly among 4 dpns. Join for working in the rnd, being careful not to twist sts; place marker (pm) for beginning of rnd. Begin Garter st (purl 1 rnd, knit 1 rnd); work even for 6 rnds.

Next Rnd: *Work Left Cable across following 12 sts, then work Right Cable across following 12 sts; repeat from * once. Work even until Cuff measures 1¾".

Next Rnd: Work 24 sts, pm, k22, pm, k2.

SIZES

Small/Medium (Large)

FINISHED MEASUREMENTS

7 ½ (8)" hand circumference

YARN

St-Denis Nordique (100% wool; 150 yards / 50 grams): 2 balls #5858 Red

NEEDLES

Size Small/Medium: One set of five double-pointed needles (dpn) size US 2 (2.75 mm)
Size Large: One set of five double-pointed needles size US 3 (3.25 mm)
Change needle size if necessary to obtain correct gauge.

NOTIONS

Cable needle (cn); stitch markers (one in contrasting color for beginning of rnd); waste yarn

GAUGE

Size Small/Medium: 13 sts and 18 rnds = 2" (5 cm) in Stockinette stitch (St st), using smaller needles
Size Large: 12 sts and 16 rnds = 2" (5 cm) in Stockinette stitch, using larger needles

Thumb Gusset

Increase Rnd: Increase 2 sts this rnd, then every 3 rnds 6 times, as follows: Work to second marker, slip marker (sm), M1-r, knit to next marker, M1-l, sm—62 sts. Work even until Thumb Gusset measures 3 (3 ¼)".

Upper Palm

Work to second marker, remove marker, place next 16 sts on waste yarn for Thumb, CO 2 sts—48 sts. Work even for 1 ¾".

Next Rnd: P24, knit to end. Knit 1 rnd.

Index Finger

K6, transfer next 36 sts to waste yarn, pm, CO 4 sts over gap, k6—16 sts. Join for working in the rnd. Continue in St st, work even for 2 ½", or to ¼" less than desired length.

Decrease Rnd 1: *K2tog; repeat from * to end—8 sts remain.

Decrease Rnd 2: *K2tog; repeat from * to end—4 sts remain. Cut yarn, leaving a 6″ tail. Thread tail though remaining sts, pull tight and fasten off.

Middle Finger

Note: Sts picked up at base of fingers are not knit when they are picked up; instead, pick up existing loops with tip of right-hand needle and place them on left-hand needle.

Transfer next 6 sts from waste yarn to Needle 1. Transfer last 6 sts from waste yarn to Needle 2. Pick up 5 sts at base of Index Finger with Needle 3; slip last 2 picked-up sts to Needle 1. Rejoin yarn; pm for beginning of rnd.

Next Rnd: K1, k2tog, k5, CO 4 sts over gap, k5, ssk, k2—19 sts. Redistribute sts. Work even for 2 ¾", or to ¼" less than desired length.

Decrease Rnd 1: *K2tog; repeat from * to last st, k1—10 sts remain.

Decrease Rnd 2: *K2tog; repeat from * to end—5 sts remain. Cut yarn, leaving a 6″ tail. Thread tail though remaining sts, pull tight and fasten off.

Ring Finger

Transfer next 6 sts from waste yarn to Needle 1. Transfer last 6 sts from waste yarn to Needle 2. Pick up 5 sts at base of Middle Finger with Needle 3; slip last 2 sts to Needle 1. Rejoin yarn; pm for beginning of rnd.

Next Rnd: K1, k2tog, k5, CO 3 sts over gap, k5, ssk, k2—18 sts. Redistribute sts. Work even for 2 ½", or to ¼" less than desired length.

Decrease Rnd 1: *K2tog; repeat from * to end—9 sts remain.

Decrease Rnd 2: *K2tog; repeat from * to last st, k1—5 sts remain. Cut yarn, leaving a 6″ tail. Thread tail though remaining sts, pull tight and fasten off.

Little Finger

Transfer remaining 12 sts evenly from waste yarn to Needles 1 and 2. Pick up 4 sts at base of Ring Finger with Needle 3; slip last 2 sts to Needle 1. Rejoin yarn; pm for beginning of rnd.

Next Rnd: K1, k2tog, k10, ssk, k1—14 sts remain. Redistribute sts. Work even for 1 ¾", or to ¼" less than desired length.

Decrease Rnd 1: *K2tog; repeat from * to end—7 sts remain.

Decrease Rnd 2: *K2tog; repeat from * to last st, k1—4 sts remain. Cut yarn, leaving a 6″ tail. Thread tail though remaining sts, pull tight and fasten off.

Thumb

Transfer 16 Thumb sts from waste yarn to Needles 1, 2, and 3. Pick up 3 sts from base of Thumb with Needle 3; slip last st to Needle 1—19 sts. Rejoin yarn; pm for beginning of rnd.

Next Rnd: K2tog, knit to last 3 sts, ssk, k1—17 sts. Work even for 2″, or to ¼" less than desired length.

Decrease Rnd 1: *K2tog; repeat from * to last st, k1—9 sts remain.

Decrease Rnd 2: *K2tog; repeat from * to last st, k1—5 sts remain. Cut yarn, leaving a 6″ tail. Thread tail through remaining sts, pull tight and fasten off.

RIGHT GLOVE
Work as for Left Glove until Cuff measures 1 ¾″.

Next Rnd: Work 24 sts, pm, k2, pm, knit to end.

Thumb Gusset
Increase Rnd: Increase 2 sts this rnd, then every 3 rnds 6 times as follows: Work to first marker, slip marker (sm), M1-r, knit to next marker, M1-l, sm, work to end—62 sts. Work even until Thumb Gusset measures 3 (3 ¼)″.

Upper Palm
Work to first marker, remove marker, place next 16 sts on waste yarn for Thumb, CO 2 sts, work to end—48 sts remain. Work even for 1 ¾".

Next Rnd: K24, purl to end. Knit 1 rnd.

Next Rnd: Remove beginning of rnd marker; k24. Work Fingers as for Left Glove.

FINISHING
Block as desired.

appendix

SPECIAL TECHNIQUES

I-Cord   Using a double-pointed needle, cast on or pick up the required number of stitches; the working yarn will be at the left-hand side of the needle. *Transfer needle with stitches to your left hand, bring yarn around behind the work to the right-hand side; using a second double-pointed needle, knit stitches from right to left, pulling yarn from left to right for the first stitch; do not turn. Slide stitches to opposite end of needle; repeat from * until the I-Cord is desired length. *Note: After a few rows, the tubular shape will become apparent.*

Kitchener Stitch (joining live stitches to live stitches)   Using a blunt tapestry needle, thread a length of yarn approximately 4 times the length of the section to be joined. Hold the pieces to be joined wrong sides together, with the needles holding the stitches parallel, both ends pointing to the right. Working from right to left, insert tapestry needle into first stitch on front needle as if to purl, pull yarn through, leaving stitch on needle; insert tapestry needle into first stitch on back needle as if to knit, pull yarn through, leaving stitch on needle; *insert tapestry needle into first stitch on front needle as if to knit, pull yarn through, remove stitch from needle; insert tapestry needle into next stitch on front needle as if to purl, pull yarn through, leave stitch on needle; insert tapestry needle into first stitch on back needle as if to purl, pull yarn through, remove stitch from needle; insert tapestry needle into next stitch on back needle as if to knit, pull yarn through, leave stitch on needle. Repeat from *, working 3 or 4 stitches at a time, then go back and adjust tension to match the pieces being joined. When 1 stitch remains on each needle, cut yarn and pass through last 2 stitches to fasten off.

Kitchener Stitch (joining live stitches to a finished edge)   Using a blunt tapestry needle, thread a length of yarn approximately 4 times the length of the section to be joined. Hold the pieces to be joined parallel to one another with their right sides facing. Working from right to left, insert tapestry needle into first stitch on front needle as if to purl, pull yarn through, leaving stitch on needle; *insert tapestry needle between first two side stitches of finished edge as if mattress stitching and pull yarn through; insert tapestry needle into first stitch on front needle as if to knit, pull yarn through, remove stitch from needle; insert tapestry needle into next stitch on front needle as if to purl, pull yarn through, leave stitch on needle; Repeat from *, working 3 or 4 stitches at a time, then go back and adjust tension to match the pieces being joined. When 1 stitch remains on needle, cut yarn and pass through last stitch to fasten off. *Note: It may be necessary to adjust the ratios of stitches to rows; count the number of running threads between the two side stitches before beginning and adjust accordingly.*

Reading Charts   Unless otherwise specified in the instructions, when working straight, charts are read from right to left for right side rows, from left to right for wrong side rows. Row numbers are written at the beginning of each row. Numbers on the right indicate right side rows; numbers on the left indicate wrong side rows. When working circular, all rounds are read from right to left.

Short Row Shaping   Work the number of stitches specified in the instructions, wrap and turn (wrp-t) as follows:

To wrap a knit stitch, bring yarn to the front (purl position), slip the next stitch purlwise to the right-hand needle, bring yarn to the back of work, return slipped stitch on right-hand needle to left-hand needle purlwise; turn, ready to work the next row, leaving remaining stitches unworked. To wrap a purl stitch, work as for wrapping a knit stitch, but bring yarn to the back (knit position) before slipping the stitch, and to the front after slipping the stitch.

When short rows are completed, or when working progressively longer short rows, work the wrap together with the wrapped stitch as you come to it as follows:

If stitch is to be worked as a knit stitch, insert right-hand needle into wrap from below, then into wrapped stitch; k2tog. If stitch to be worked is a purl stitch, insert needle into wrapped stitch, then down into wrap; p2tog. (Wrap may be lifted onto the left-hand needle, then worked together with the wrapped stitch if this is easier.)

Steeks   A steek is a field of extra stitches that is inserted when working the Stranded (Fair Isle) Method in the round; it will be cut after the piece is finished, e.g., for the front of a cardigan. These stitches are not usually included in the stitch count. Work and cut as instructed in the text. When picking up stitches after cutting a steek, pick up between the last (first) steek stitch and the first (last) pattern stitch; the steek stitches will turn to the wrong side. To finish, trim the steek stitches and whipstitch to the wrong side.

Stem Stitch BO   Cut yarn, leaving a tail approximately 4 to 5 times the length of the edge to be bound off. Thread tail onto tapestry needle. Working from left to right, *insert tapestry needle into second stitch from front, then into first stitch from back, then pull yarn through; drop first stitch from needle; repeat from * until 1 stitch remains. Thread tail through remaining stitch and fasten off.

Stranded (Fair Isle) Colorwork Method   When more than one color is used per row, carry color(s) not in use loosely across wrong side of work. Be sure to secure all colors at beginning and end of rows to prevent holes.

Three-Needle BO   Place stitches to be joined onto two same-size needles; hold pieces to be joined with right sides facing each other and needles parallel, both pointing to the right. Holding both needles in your left hand, using working yarn and a third needle same size or one size larger, insert third needle into first stitch on front needle, then into first stitch on back needle; knit these 2 stitches together; * knit next stitch from each needle together (2 stitches on right-hand needle); pass first stitch over second stitch to bind off 1 stitch. Repeat from * until 1 stitch remains on third needle; cut yarn and fasten off.

Yarn Over (yo)   Bring yarn forward (to the purl position), then place it in position to work the next stitch. If next stitch is to be knit, bring yarn over the needle and knit; if next stitch is to be purled, bring yarn over the needle and then forward again to the purl position and purl. Work the yarnover in pattern on the next row unless instructed otherwise.

ABBREVIATIONS

BO   Bind off

Ch   Chain

Circ   Circular

Cn   Cable needle

CO   Cast on

Dpn(s)   Double-pointed needle(s)

K   Knit

K1b   Knit 1 into st below st on left-hand needle.

K1-f/b   Knit into front loop and back loop of same st to increase 1 st.

K1-tbl   Knit 1 st through back loop.

K2tog   Knit 2 sts together.

K3tog   Knit 3 sts together.

M1 or M1-l (make 1-left slanting) With tip of left-hand needle inserted from front to back, lift strand between 2 needles onto left-hand needle; knit strand through back loop to increase 1 st.

M1-r (make 1-right slanting)   With tip of left-hand needle inserted from back to front, lift strand between 2 needles onto left-hand needle; knit strand through front loop to increase 1 st.

P   Purl

P2tog   Purl 2 sts together.

P3tog   Purl 3 sts together.

Pm   Place marker.

Psso (pass slipped st over)   Pass slipped st on right-hand needle over sts indicated in instructions, as in binding off.

Rnd(s)   Round(s)

RS(s)   Right side(s)

S2kp2   Slip next 2 sts together to right-hand needle as if to knit 2 together, k1, pass 2 slipped sts over.

Skp (slip, knit, pass)   Slip next st knitwise to right-hand needle, k1, pass slipped st over knit st.

Sk2p (double decrease)   Slip next st knitwise to right-hand needle, k2tog, pass slipped st over st from k2tog.

Sm   Slip marker.

Ssk (slip, slip, knit)   Slip next 2 sts to right-hand needle one at a time as if to knit; return them to left-hand needle one at a time in their new orientation; knit them together through back loops.

Ssp (slip, slip, purl)   Slip next 2 sts to right-hand needle one at a time as if to knit; return them to left-hand needle one at a time in their new orientation; purl them together through back loops.

St(s)   Stitch(es)

Tbl   Through the back loop

Tog   Together

WS(s)   Wrong side(s)

Wrp-t   Wrap and turn (see Special Techniques—Short Row Shaping)

Wyib   With yarn in back

Wyif   With yarn in front

Yo   Yarnover (see Special Techniques)

YARN SOURCES

Berroco, Inc.
14 Elmdale Road
PO Box 367
Uxbridge, MA 01569
508-278-2527
www.berroco.com

Cascade Yarns
1224 Andover Park East
Tukwila, WA 98188
800-548-1048
www.cascadeyarns.com
(Distributed in Canada by Estelle Yarns)

Classic Elite Yarns
122 Western Avenue
Lowell, MA 01851
800-343-0308
www.classiceliteyarns.com
(Distributed in Canada by
The Old Mill Knitting Company)

Dale of Norway, Inc.
4750 Shelburne Road, Suite 20
Shelburne, VT 05482
802-383-0132
www.dale.no
(Distributed in Canada by Estelle Yarns)

Estelle Yarns
2220 Midland Avenue, Unit 65
Scarborough, Ontario, Canada M1P 3E6
416-298-9922
www.estelleyarns.com

Fiddlesticks Knitting
3 Graham Gardens
Toronto, Ontario, Canada M6C 1G6
888-229-3711
www.fiddlesticksknitting.com

Garnstudio
(Distributed by Nordic Yarn Imports Ltd.)
#301 5327 192nd Street
Surrey, British Columbia, Canada V3S 8E5
800-663-0008
www.nordicyarn.ca

Handmaiden Fine Yarn
Halifax, Nova Scotia, Canada
www.handmaiden.ca

Harrisville Designs
Center Village, PO Box 806
Harrisville, NH 03450
800-338-9415
www.harrisville.com

Jaggerspun
5 Water Street
Springvale, ME 04083
207-324-4455
www.jaggeryarn.com

Kid Hollow Farm
PO Box 101
Free Union, VA 22940
434-973-8070
www.kidhollow.com

Kraemer Yarns
PO Box 72
Nazareth, PA 18064
800-759-5601
www.kraemeryarns.com

Lanaknits Designs
Suite 3B, 320 Vernon Street
Nelson, British Columbia,
Canada V1L 4E4
888-301-0011
www.lanaknits.com

Louet Sales
808 Commerce Park Drive
Ogdensburg, NY 13669
613-925-4502
www.louet.com

Manos del Uruguay
(Distributed by Fairmount Fibers)
915 North 28th Street
Philadelphia, PA 19130
888-566-9970
www.fairmountfibers.com

Nashua Handknits
(Distributed by Westminster Fibers)
4 Townsend West, Unit 8
Nashua, NH 03063
603-886-5041
www.knitrowan.com

Naturally
(Distributed by Fiber Trends)
315 Colorado Park Place
PO Box 7266
East Wenatchee, WA 98802
509-884-8631
www.fibertrends.com
(Distributed in Canada by
The Old Mill Knitting Company)

The Old Mill Knitting Company
F.G. PO Box 81176
Ancaster, Ontario, Canada L9G 4X2
905-648-3483
www.oldmillknitting.com

Peace Fleece
475 Porterfield Road
Porter, ME 04068
207-625-4906
www.peacefleece.com

Rowan
(Distributed by Westminster Fibers)
4 Townsend West, Unit 8
Nashua, NH 03063
603-886-5041
www.knitrowan.com

Schaefer Yarn Company
3514 Kelly's Corners Road
Interlaken, NY 14847
607-532-9452
www.schaeferyarn.com

Schoeller + Stahl
(Distributed by Skacel Collection Inc.)
PO Box 88110
Seattle, WA 98138
800-255-1278
www.skacelknitting.com

St-Denis Yarns
2273 Harvard Avenue
Montreal, Quebec, Canada H4A 2WI
514-652-5648
www.stdenisyarns.com
(Distributed in the U.S.A.
by Classic Elite Yarns)

ACKNOWLEDGMENTS

It's hard to put into words my gratitude to those who have made this book possible. I'd like to begin by thanking my friends Pam Allen, Robin Melanson, Carol Sulcoski, Julia Grunau, Laura Grutzeck, and Shannon Shields—even though we don't get to talk as often as we'd like, each conversation picks up as though we left off the day before.

The local knitting community in Montreal has always welcomed me when I need to run away from my desk, and I am thankful that I have been able to join them on many Wednesday evenings on Monkland Avenue.

Thanks go to the skillful knitters who helped me create the samples (and always with good spirit): Jonathan Ayers, Sarah Ayers, Jennifer Carpman, Erin Clark, Janet Faith, Andrea Hig, Alison Jacques, Karine Louis-Jacques, Janet Lum, Laura May, and Leslie Ordal.

Thanks also to Thayer Gowdy for the photography, Karen Schaupeter for the styling, and Anna Christian for the book's design. This book wouldn't be what it is without them. I am grateful to Melanie Falick and Liana Allday for their editorial support and guidance, as well as to Sue McCain for her technical editing skills.

Thanks also go to my family for their love, support, and understanding. But most of all, thanks to Marcel and Oona—I can't imagine life without you.

Photography Credits
Hair and Makeup: Diane da Silva and Vincent Oquendo
Scouting: Rob Lee
Production Assistant: Brian Stevens
Talent: Eva Kass, Georgina, and Jennifer Beaty (from Q Management), and Bobbi Misick.
Locations: Nicolette Camille Floral Design (nicolettecamille.com), Marlow & Daughters, Biography Bookshop, Butter Lane Cupcakes, Landmark Vintage Bicycles, and No. 7 restaurant